WHAT ARE THEY SAYING ABOUT
THE GRACE OF CHRIST?

What Are They Saying About the Grace of Christ?

Brian O. McDermott, S.J.

PAULIST PRESS
New York/Ramsey

Imprimi potest
Edward M. O'Flaherty, S.J.
Provincial, Society of Jesus of New England
March 21, 1983

Copyright © 1984 by
Brian O. McDermott, S.J.

Library of Congress
Catalog Card Number: 83-62017

ISBN: 0-8091-2584-6

Published by Paulist Press
545 Island Road, Ramsey, N.J. 07446

Printed and bound in the
United States of America

Contents

Preface   1

1. Grace and Culture   5

2. Grace as Acceptance   12

3. Grace as Conversion   21

4. Grace as Discipleship in Community   35

5. Grace as Witness and Service   48

6. Prospects for the Theology of Grace   59

   Notes   66

   Selected Bibliography   69

Preface

Modern developments in the human sciences have helped us pay much more attention to the dynamics of human development as a psychological, moral and religious process. Erik Erikson's work is preeminent in this regard, but other names are also significant: Lawrence Kohlberg, Daniel Levinson, Donald Evans, James Fowler, Carol Gilligan and Robert Kegan.[1] Their attention to the human life-cycle makes it clear that, for all the variety among people in a given culture, there is an almost organic quality to the sequence of phases that they will undergo if they are able to continue to mature and meet crises. The basic pattern usually involves the initial establishment of an atmosphere of trust and trustworthiness fostered by the parental and family environment, which then allows the individual to develop a sense of self, a development which in turn makes it possible to enter into a more and more adventuresome engagement with an increasingly larger world while negotiating the crises of intimacy and generativity along the way.

The theologian of grace can also discern a pattern to the process of Christian identity. This discernment rests on the conviction that God's self-communication to persons is a conscious process in some sense, and that it touches deeply into the most fundamental dynamisms of the human person as a seeker for personal meaning and as a builder of culture. There is nothing rigid about this pattern, and no individual's development in Christian identity can be predicted or made to fit into some kind of procrustean bed. Nonetheless, there is direction in the growth of a truly Christian personality. The theologian, when reflecting on the effect of God's self-communication in human lives, tries to be attentive to that orientedness. Human growth is always a matter of the organic and the free, and when we are dealing with God's relationship with creatures we are concerned with two freedoms, the Creator's and the finite creature's. Moreover, the individual Christian or the community of Christians, when naming their crucial or threshold moments, may well be explicitly aware of one moment occurring before another; yet the theologian, in delineating a sequence of phases, may want to maintain that a certain individual or group implicitly experienced another moment as basis for the threshold or critical moment that is the first one named. For theology draws on the experience of the whole community as well as on that of individuals, and this means that descriptions of experience will not always tally between theology and an individual life-history.

In this exploration of the theology of grace, I shall not be attempting to correlate the development of Christian identity as a gracious process with the life cycle as discussed by Erikson and others, but rather I shall consider growth in the life of grace as a spiral with a direction, the goal being the eschatological completion in Christ symbolized by the resurrection of the body. Each Christian, while he or she is still a pilgrim, shares in each of these phases of Christian identity, but at every time in our lives we are being invited to mature in a focused way in one of the phases or to pass beyond into another phase as the place of development. Obviously, active engagement in this process depends very much on the degree of attentiveness that a person or a group is able to bring to their lives. John Dunne reminds us that being an embodied spirit means that the human being can consciously relate to the mystery of his or her life as a whole;[2] thus, the degree of our spiritual alertness, rooted in God's grace, determines how much we are able to learn from our own experience of God's gift.

Traditional theology divided the notion of grace into a whole series of sub-notions. While distinguishing is still part of the theologian's craft, the emphasis in contemporary theology has shifted. More attention goes now to relating the scriptural and traditional approaches to grace to humanity's quest for God in religious experience. The stock-in-trade of classical theology's discussion of grace was the use of terms and distinctions which were part of the catechetical education of every Catholic: justification and sanctification, habitual and actual grace, the state of grace, the theological virtues, attrition and contrition, the notion of merit, the supernatural, nature and grace, original justice and the preternatural gifts.

In this volume the distinctions of classical theology will have their role to play, but the accent will fall on a synthetic rather than an analytic approach to the mystery of grace. Authors such as Karl Rahner, Edward Schillebeeckx, Sebastian Moore, and Hans Kung will nourish our reflections. Their contributions to a renewed understanding of grace will be presented in a way which allows us to see the life of grace as a life process involving phases of development, and even more mysteriously involving God's freedom for us and our response in freedom to God, others and ourselves. Furthermore, we shall come to appreciate how contemporary Christology contributes to a dynamic understanding of grace. For grace is not only a gift from Christ but his very identity as well.

1 Grace and Culture

The theology of grace can seem a very ambitious enterprise. It seems to encompass all of theology, exploring as it does the mystery of God, the event of Jesus Christ, the existence of the Church and indeed the very meaning of human beings in a contingent world blessed by God. Because human existence is, among other things, a marvelous and threatening mixture of gift and achievement, of celebration and hard work, it might be helpful, before examining the dynamics of grace as a life-process, to look first at two important connections: the connection between theology and culture, that most pervasive of human achievements, and the connection between theology and God's self-communication, God's greatest gift.

Theology and Culture

In its most basic sense, culture is the effort of human beings, socially and personally, to organize the chaos of stimuli which bombard human organisms in a way that will allow them to function in this world productively and healthily. Because we humans enter the world bereft of animal instincts which, if present, would fit us to live in a limited ecological niche, we desperately need education from our environment about the booming, buzzing world that throws in our direction—unasked—thousands of conflicting stimuli.

Culture is that intricate web of learned responses to the world which we enter, gradually yielding to its charms and self-evident character at the same time that we feel, way down deep, that we are each called to stand apart, distinct, from this womb or milieu that gave us our first identity. Ernest Becker has shown us that culture is both an effort of men and women to stymie the life-threatening avalanche of stimuli, and at the same time the heroic expression of a people's desire to fashion a special identity and a destiny for themselves.[3] Through culture we shape our response to life and death, to sexuality and aggression, to nature as a given and as a material to be humanized, to the Unknown which doesn't diminish, but seems to recede before culture's advance.

A profound disequilibrium in the heart of the individual human person and of human societies lies at the root of culture. For we are bodies that grow, decay and die, and simultaneously we are beings who can transcend our bodies, our culture and our world by symbolizing ourselves, our world and the Unknown that surrounds us as an ambiguous Presence. As Pascal wrote centuries ago, we are glorious in our knowledge of our frailty and vulnerability, and all the more vulnerable because of that self-knowledge. Thus culture is that personal and social achievement that arises out of both our prerogative as human beings and our deep-rooted anxiety. Prerogative: we are made to be special, unique, *and* to belong to the mysterious Whole. Anxiety: our basic dynamism toward both independence and dependence can and often does crucify us in the very ambitioning of both these "natural" human values. We are fraught with paradox precisely here. To intensify our identity or the identity of the group on which we lean, we say a powerful "no" to many stimuli and invitations coming from within and without. Yet to make up for the scary contingency we find in ourselves we seek to merge with another creature and to surrender to it, denying its limits and our capacity for more than that nation, ideology, god, gang or lover can possibly deliver. Culture is the most human of achievements, expressive of all that is most substantial and transcendent about us human creators of meanings, yet culture remains the revealer of our deepest vulnerability, precisely as human beings.

The relationship between culture and religion is thus a very special one. Not only is religion in most societies part of the warp and woof of their culture, but it expresses the society's recognition of and response to both the creative, transcendent energies present in that society and the experiences of limit which shape and challenge that human community. And those limits are many: biological destiny, the indifference and violence of nature, the power and mystery of sexuality, the aggression of humans against humans, and finally death, both individual and collective. Because culture and religion are so deeply intertwined, theology has everything to do with culture.

Bernard Lonergan sees theology mediating between a religion and a culture.[4] By interpreting the religious experience of a people, theologians try to understand the relevance of the symbols, doctrines, and rituals of a religion to the changing culture, and also the bearing of that culture on the religion. Surely Christian theology, when healthy, has attempted to welcome and critically examine this reciprocal relationship. For example, when the Black Death and the disintegration of the medieval world-order stripped European Christians of their familiar mediators between God and their daily lives (mediators in the form of trustworthy civil structures, credible priests, or religious institutions such as indulgences which linked the living and the dead in reassuring ways), a Martin Luther emerged who passed through this experience of deprivation, of living naked and defenseless before the Holy Mystery, and was able to give voice to that experience for countless others. Thus a new culture and a new religious form took shape, partly due to Luther's immense influence. The theologies of the Reformers, for all their important differences, bear common witness to a need to mediate between a new Europe and a new religious experience. At present, we can observe the beginnings in the Roman Catholic Church of a world-Church, which, according to Karl Rahner, is the primary fruit of the Second Vatican Council.[5] This watershed in the history of the Church is matched only by the early move from Jewish Christianity to Gentile Christianity. Theologies which interpret and foster this emergence will be mediating between indigenous religious experience in different areas of the world and the cultures—African, Asian, Latin American—which are growing more autonomous at the same time that they are challenged to newer forms of interdependence.

Christian theology is vitally concerned with the human project that is called "culture," precisely because, as we have seen, culture gives expression to what is most basic in us humans, the drive to be unique and special and the dynamism to belong to a larger, meaning-bestowing whole. The creativity and anxiety that reside in all human persons and societies are the concern of Christian theology because the religious experience of Christians is experience of all human life touched and changed by God in Christ and the Spirit. In Christianity, uniqueness (the desire to be special) and universality (the desire to belong to the Whole) meet in Jesus Christ and his relation, in the Holy Spirit, to the universe of matter and persons and to the life of God. The project of human life—to be autonomous as well as capable of life-giving surrender—acquires a name in Christianity, both personal (Jesus) and familial (Church). For Christians know Jesus Christ as the definitive revelation of both God's true reality and our own true identity as human beings in community. Christian theology has everything to do with this God-granted revelation, just as it has everything to do with culture.

Theology and God's Self-Communication

Revelation as a religious term often initially suggests to people the notion of a truth becoming disclosed which previously was hidden—a veil removed so that someone might come to see or know. In contemporary Roman Catholic theology, represented by Karl Rahner, God's revelation of the divine being is spoken of as God's *self-communication* to the world through Christ in the power of the Holy Spirit.[6] The accent falls here on God's giving God away to the created universe, a self-giving which makes God to be grace for us, or, as the older tradition expressed it, God as Uncreated Grace. Latin or Western theology, Rahner writes, did not maintain the centrality of Uncreated Grace, and in this respect has differed significantly from Eastern theologians who have seen in God's self-gift to us the primary meaning of grace. In Christ and the Spirit, Rahner maintains, we meet God's self-emptying toward us and for our sakes. And he will insist that the *entire purpose* of creation is that God might be grace for us, to God's glory.

This viewpoint on the matter can be succinctly put: creation is grounded in, motivated by, God's total graciousness. Not that God *must* create; not that the Holy Mystery *must* empty the divine self for the sake of creatures. Rahner avoids both of these "necessities." But we Christians can confidently and boldly confess that we *are* and all the created order exists in order that God might give God away.

Rahner goes further. God can be gift in the fullest sense only if there are beings who are fully other than God. Purely material or natural entities are not *fully* "different" from God, because they are not free, and they are not able to receive anything from God beyond their own being. Humans, however, are those worldly beings who are open to all reality with an openness that makes them human. This basic openness is human freedom in one of its most important senses. Being free, humans are really different from God, while being created by the Holy Mystery and available, so to speak, if God wants to give the divine life away.

God can become Uncreated Grace because God is free to choose to be gift and because there are beings who, because free, are possible receivers of that gift. Our basic freedom or openness to all reality concretely occurs through our knowledge and love, two basic human operations which, while distinct, are at root united. We can love only what we know, and really know only those realities we are able to love. If Christians are right that God, all along and everywhere, has been giving God away to human beings in their freedom (what Rahner calls their transcendence), then human knowing and loving is different from what it would be if this divine self-communication to the world were not going on. This does not mean that our experiences of knowing and loving are elevated from the human to some suprahuman or non-human level, but that all our conscious experience is interiorly affected by the divine gift even before we say yes or no to it, or, indeed, are explicitly conscious of the presence of the gift. Grace does not show up as an element or item in our awareness, but rather as a change, an elevation of our human transcendence, which we cannot separate off in our explicit awareness but which is distinct from the dynamism of our human nature.

But then how does this influence of the gift of divine life show up in the culture-building animal which is the human being? Rahner offers some examples, all of which are Christian interpretations of human experience in the light of an explicit awareness of grace.[7] We protest against death in its darkness and threat to our lives. Is that protest, asks Rahner, only because the human animal wants to go on living? Is it just a selfish reaction to a biological, and thus "natural," ending of our lives? Or is the protest possibly the sign as well of an ought-not-to-be aspect of death in its opaqueness and danger, because we are surrounded and interiorly touched and affected by the divine life which excludes all death? Moreover, perhaps the hope against hope which arises in people in the most absurd and dehumanizing of circumstances is not illusion but resonance in them of the divine life which is so totally close to them.

We experience emptiness and aloneness at times, and our culture, at its worst, tries to shield us from this experience. But this recognition of void is a genuinely human experience and, if we stay with it, it often shows us a strangely consoling truth about ourselves. We learn that no particular object in our experience, no person, no accumulation of objects or persons, can fill us up. That is our truth. And so we become a little more free to be with objects and persons, respecting them for their reality and limits. Is this truthful experience not rooted in an implicit sense of our being different because God's infinity is our true home?

The experience of sin, as distinct from the experience of our finitude or ability to make mistakes, is not the province of believing people only. Is not the "healthy" sense of sin a sense that our freedom is measured by nothing less than an infinitely Holy Presence which is given to us as the very atmosphere of our deepest identity?

Insofar as God's self-communication interiorly shapes and affects all human life, Rahner calls this shaping the "supernatural existential" in human life. It is an existential, because, like being-in-the-world or being-a-culture-builder, this shaping is a fundamental total dimension of being human; it is not just a region of human existence. It is supernatural insofar as it is the first fruit in us of God's utterly gratuitous self-offer. It is, therefore, in Rahner's theology, the primary or initial created grace—created because it is a dimension of our finite conscious being; grace because it is fruit of divine gift. I would venture to call this supernatural existential by another name as well: original redemptive grace, since we are qualified and shaped before we even know it explicitly by the death and resurrection of Jesus. The grace of the divine life as victoriously accepted by Christ in the Holy Spirit is our milieu. It is an existential of our very lives. Even when we reject it, it is still the horizon and atmosphere in which we live out our "hell." For Rahner, all human history is affected by this grace.

In later chapters we shall consider the ways in which Uncreated Grace—the living God as God among us and in us—affects human development, but for the present it is sufficient to see how contemporary theology recognizes the human condition as everywhere a graced condition affecting all conscious life, at least pre-conceptually or implicitly. The human dynamism to be individual or special and the dynamism to belong to a larger Whole are radical dimensions of human living which God's self-communication meets, transforms, and consummates in the twofold gift which the New Testament celebrates: the forgiveness of sin for the sake of participation in the divine life. Culture and grace, though not simply identical, are ineluctably intertwined. Culture, as the glory, sin and terrifying ambiguity of the human project, is the most public way in which the human creature responds to, rejects, toys with or flees from the divine offer of conversion and completion. The goodness of the project as human, and the perversion of the project as sin, both come to light as real goodness and deathly sin only through God's self-communication. The magnitude of our goodness and guilt are uncovered in their deepest truth no other way. Our goodness and guilt show their real stuff only when they rub against the presence of Uncreated Grace dwelling among us.

2 Grace as Acceptance

At the heart of human life an offer is being made that can only come from God. This offer is "too good to be true," beyond our just deserts. It has something about it that marks it as different from everything that our human and natural world is able to give to us. This gift is divine, yet it comes to us most often through the words and deeds of other human beings. It is unconditional; it meets us as we are and asks only to be accepted, but it arrives in our lives mediated by the very conditioned love and concern of others for us. It is the divine gift of unconditional acceptance. Sometimes this gift enters our lives in a dramatic fashion, with a signal loud and clear. For other people it is a dim but precious experience as though "through a glass darkly." In other cases it is the memory of an experience which nourishes present faith and hope.

This gift, which is the most fundamental offer that God makes to his creatures, is difficult to receive and accept, because it invites a level of trust which goes deeper than we are usually willing to travel. Yet the beginnings of such trust are very human ones. Developmental psychologists point out that an infant, born into the world, is particularly vulnerable because instincts do not determine its life. The dependency of the infant on the mother is complete, and the offered acceptance of the child on the part of the mother allows the young one to develop trust in the mother, its environment and itself. The mother, as it were, trusts for the child, until gradually the child is able to recognize that the world, thanks to its mother or significant other, is a *basically* reliable world.

Christians are convinced that in and through all such experiences of human acceptance and trust (and indeed, even in contrast experiences of rejection and distrust) God is communicating an acceptance of humankind that is more than, in excess of, the human words and gestures of acceptance. These hint at and give partial expression to the divine acceptance which is utterly reliable; this reliability is known in the very trusting in it. There is a circularity here. The trust is fruit of the acceptance received, yet the acceptance is experienced only by entering into it. As Karl Rahner expresses it, the deepest truths are the freest.[8] The truth that is life-giving for the whole person is knowable only to the degree that the person surrenders to it wholly, while partial truths, such as mathematics, are knowable if only a part of ourselves becomes involved.

This unconditional acceptance is God's yes to creation, God's "It is good," which is said creatively to all that is not God because and insofar as it is God's creation. This acceptance is more than God's creation of a creature (although it surely is that too) because the yes said by God is not simply identical with the creature's being; it is God's self-gift to the creature in divine self-communication. It is a message which comes to the creature from beyond itself; it is not a word produced by us or at our disposal, but one which comes as incalculable surprise and gift. The gift of acceptance is not a set of words resounding in the mind; it is not a particular item of human consciousness at all. Rahner speaks of it as an attunement or tonality of our spiritual self-consciousness, not known as an object is known, but known affectively along with knowledge of persons and things of this world.

If we allow the divine message of acceptance to come through to us, something else occurs. Theologians speak of this aspect of the acceptance experience as the experience of the creature's intrinsic acceptability as gift. This is technical language for a subtle but very important dimension of the process by which God's acceptance "seeps into" us. It calls for some explanation.

Acceptance is sheer gift, not at all arbitrary or capricious, but pure gift nonetheless. This acceptance reaches down into people, so to speak, and seeks their reception of the gift. The divine gift is telling them, deep in their spiritual identity, that they are accepted by God, just as they are, unconditionally, prior to any decisions to reform their lives, pay their bills or seek reconciliation with an enemy. But God's accepting people this way reveals to them that they are intrinsically—in themselves—*able* to be accepted. God has accepted them *and* this very acceptability is also being communicated as gift to them as God's creatures oriented to such a gift. That is why it is best to speak of this dimension as intrinsic-acceptability-as-gift.

Two contrasting and extreme views of the human self before the accepting God will help reveal what is at stake here. On the one hand, there is a strand of religious interpretation which would express the experience this way: "I am junk, but God accepts me unconditionally; still I am junk, but, juxtaposed to that, God keeps on accepting me unconditionally." The opposite extreme puts it this way: "I am unconditionally accepted and loved by God, so that in, of, and by myself I am intrinsically acceptable and can now expand that goodness by my own good deeds and sufferings." This first position is a caricature of certain understandings of the Protestant principle of "simul justus et peccator" (at once just and sinner), while the second view is a distortion of a Catholic understanding of grace and creation. Each view errs because in neither case is the point understood that God's free communication of acceptance to the creature (a) is constant and continual gift received as such by the creature, and (b) includes the gifting of the creature with acceptability, with a capacity for the gift which is identical with the creature's being oriented all along by God to this gift. Both the divine acceptance and the human acceptability are divine gift: gift meets gift. Simple juxtaposition of sin and acceptance is not the Christian sense of things; neither is a flaccid view of the acceptability of the creature in God's eye as a human possession or achievement. We are acceptable and accepted because and insofar as God gives us both human being and divine life.

This gift of acceptance and of intrinsic acceptability empowers the person who receives it to awaken to the beginnings of a new relationship to self, God and others, perceived a little more *as they are,* and not as projections of the sinful ego. This responsive acceptance on my part is but a beginning; it is the giving of space to others, to self, to God, a basic yes, a fundamental, freshly minted love for self, God and others, which can pave the way for further maturation in the Spirit. But it is the principle and foundation, source and basis of all that follows. We now turn to a consideration of Jesus' story to see the element of acceptance at work there.

Jesus as Parable of God's Acceptance

All through the ministry of the pre-Easter Jesus, as contemporary Christology highlights features of his activity among people, Jesus constantly received all that he was from the Father in the Holy Spirit. In the depths of Jesus' being, the Father spoke a "yes" to Jesus of unconditional acceptance. While the New Testament authors show little interest in the religious psychology of Jesus, we do have several stories of pivotal events in Jesus' life, in which the Father, with the Spirit, declares the divine favor which rests on Jesus, the stories of the baptism by John and the transfiguration. In each of these narratives, God has the primary initiative, revealing Jesus' God-given identity as Son and Beloved. Jesus' invocation of the God of Israel as Abba, a name suggesting a new and daring intimacy with the Father of Israel, Jesus' evocation of the symbol of the Kingdom in his preaching, and his consorting with the "unacceptable" with an apparently sovereign understanding of who he was before God, all point to a principle-and-foundation experience in Jesus' life that wasn't the matter of a moment or special hour, but a persistent feature of his experience of God. At the root of his life and work Jesus received a yes from God which was unmanipulable, mysterious (i.e., full of God's mystery) and creative in Jesus' humanity of an intrinsic acceptability and a joyous acceptance of God his Father, of himself as dearly loved and of others as also loved unconditionally by the same Holy Mystery.

The gift which Jesus receives from the Divine Other in his life is so much *his* (yet his as constant gift to him) that he is able to communicate what he has received to others. He becomes a parable of God's gracious acceptance. If we observe Jesus' behavior with fellow Jews we can see how grace was effective in and through Jesus for others.

Sebastian Moore sees Jesus relating to the guilt-ridden, to the demoniacs and the sick, to the self-righteous, and finally to children.[9]

The guilt-ridden, such as tax collectors, experience themselves as unaccepted by their religious sisters and brothers, and unaccepted and unacceptable even to their families and themselves. Their identities are so eaten away by guilt that they come to expect nothing from themselves but evil: "I am wicked, and so what else can you expect from me! Here I go again, documenting the truth about myself with more of the same." This vicious spiral of guilt-riddenness can only be subverted by a creative word from outside the spiral which, entering, communicates an acceptance that comes as alluring and fresh gift. Awakened to a long-lost sense of goodness, the publican or prostitute is brought to a new beginning of acceptance and acceptability. This is not *creatio a nihilo* (sheer creation out of nothing), but a communication which restores to the person the original relation to self, God and others which guilt has distorted beyond recognition. The worth that the creature has as God's good creature and which secretly is known by the creature, but in a distorted, self-centered manner, is liberated in an initial way as the freely-offered word of acceptance works its way into the guilty person's consciousness.

Viewing Jesus' first strategy with the guilt-ridden as the communication of unconditional acceptance permits us to appreciate the power inherent in his invitation to publicans and prostitutes to dine with him under the sign of God's Kingdom. Jesus, I think, is first saying by this gesture, "God accepts you, and so do I— just as you are, in your creaturely goodness and self-destructiveness." The invitation he proffers, in other words, is not first of all an explicit offer of forgiveness, because they are not yet on the way to wanting forgiveness. That will come later. First, Jesus lovingly "subverts" the guilty by getting to them under the dark armor, so to speak, of their accustomed guilt-riddenness.

Demoniacs and sick people in Jesus' day were in desperate need of acceptance, for they were caught in a culture which assumed that such conditions were a sign of God's disfavor. Rejected by the community, they were lost in self-rejection which closed out life-giving relationships to God and others. By his touch and look of love, Jesus penetrated the prison they were caught in, and restored a sense of God-gifted worth to them that helped free them from their plight.

The self-righteous are a different breed. They are gifted, and they can name their gifts, good deeds and honorable omissions. The armor they carry around is in some respects tougher to penetrate than the thick skin of the guilt-ridden. For the latter are hurting (in an unhelpful sort of way) but the self-righteous have taken the measure of the divine and the human and know, or think they know, just where they stand. The self-righteous among the Pharisees (but surely not restricted to them) use their real goodness and gifts as tools of self-maintenance and self-justification, thus protecting themselves from the mystery and non-manipulability of sheer grace. In order to reach the heart of the hypocrites, Jesus must employ various stratagems. He can try to trap them by parables; he can representatively mourn their spiritual deadness; he can, if all else fails, lovingly denounce them, with the hope that, pounding on their armor, he might stir up some real life inside that armor. As Moore suggests, he will even try to promote them to being sinners (cf Mt 5:28), not to add guilt feelings to self-righteousness, but to make them vulnerable to gift, to acceptance as God's creative word that is life for men and women.

Finally, there were the children. Jesus simply loved to be with them, implicitly saying a yes to them that promised more than their culture, or parents, or their incipient self-assertiveness could ever hope to provide. His agenda with them was a simple one: to be with them as God wants to be with his people, if only they would be willing to receive that gift. And children know how to receive gifts: with unfeigned eagerness.

Thus we see grace "in action" in its most basic stage, when we reverently watch Jesus in his interaction with people under the sign of the Kingdom he preached so single-mindedly. In the beginning of our responsive lives as Christians is the experience of God's acceptance, our own intrinsic acceptability as gift and our new acceptance of God, self, and the rest of God's creation. The publican, demoniac, Pharisee, and child in us experience the touch which gives life, companionship and hope for a new future.

The acceptance Jesus offered continued on the cross. He never placed himself above his crucifiers nor excluded them from his life. This acceptance on the cross could well have been a mute one, which only the resurrection would reveal in its true depth. The evangelists convey the religious dimensions of the cross in the various last words which they attribute to the dying Jesus, but not one of them expresses an exclusion or rejection of those who are killing him and thus repudiating God's offer through Jesus. Indeed, Luke is most explicit in viewing Jesus' dying as a prayer for forgiveness, which itself is grounded in a God-given attitude of total acceptance of those who are rejecting him.

After the violence of Good Friday and the emptiness of Holy Saturday, the disciples who betrayed their Master by denial and flight are met by this same Jesus, now alive in the Spirit. The first basic word spoken to these sinners is "Peace be with you." At the beginning of the life of the Church is Christ's word of unconditional acceptance of those companions who betrayed their discipleship by letting fear become their absolute.

Creation and Grace: An Ecumenical View

In order to highlight some of the differences and continuity between the classic doctrine of grace and the more recent, experientially oriented theologies, it might be helpful if we compare the recent reflections of Sebastian Moore with a modern classic, Hans Kung's *Justification, The Doctrine of Karl Barth and a Catholic Reflection.*[10] Each of these writers, for all their differences of approach and method, is interested in the affinity that exists between creation and covenant, between the human heart's deepest desire (no matter how distorted) and God's offer of divine life as offer to us of acceptance.

Moore, influenced by Christian symbols and a Jungian understanding of the psyche, as well as by his own religious experience, has come to recognize a deep desire in every human person to be someone for another. This deeply unified yet many-sided desire involves (a) the desire to be *someone*, (b) the desire to be someone and recognized as such by the other, and (c) the desire to be someone for the good of the other, which involves the other person's returning the desire. If any dimension of this rich desire becomes distorted, or is short-circuited, then the human person and the human community is in trouble.

Moore suggests that every human person is given, with the grace of creation, a "natural" love of God, others and self, these loves being the resonance in the person of God's loving the person into existence. In and through all human self-love in its destructive forms we can catch a glimpse (in the light of revelation) of a long-lost love for self which has lived on that divine love. But this self-love and love for others, this being someone for self and others, is inextricably tied up with consenting to the truth of one's creaturehood, namely, that we are totally dependent on the creating God, and that the possibility of our becoming someone and of our becoming someone for another finite reality is grounded in our existing from and for the Divine Other. Any effort to create myself as someone special and as special for another will go astray if I try to fashion my identity simply through self-maintenance and self-justification, in other words, through any deadly form of self-autonomy.

If God explicitly or implicitly comes to be seen in my deepest psyche as rival rather than source, if the finite realities around me begin to appear as extensions of my importance or as ultimate threats to my specialness, then my deepest desire, given to me graciously in God's continued creation of me, becomes thwarted and perverted. Then the energy God gives me to become someone for another becomes energy used *against* the other, and against the Divine Other. Desire on this level is not, at root, wrong, because it is part of my God-given nature, but its perversion is a total one because perversion of this desire is perversion of who I am as creature.

Thus, for Moore, the first "message" that I need to receive as pure gift given to the deepest recesses of the self, is the message from the Divine Other that I am accepted and loved, that I am and can become someone-for-the-Other even in my perversion of that deep dynamism, that "dearest freshness deep down" in me. This is precisely the message that God communicates to the self-righteous and guilt-ridden in the divine self-communication. I am distorted and perverted in my deepest, identifying desire, but God chooses to be for me right *there,* right where I am contradicting myself, and polluting that "dearest freshness." This acceptance is not, of course, a yes said to the destructiveness of my distorted desire. God loves me too much to do that. But it is emphatically a yes said to *me* as creature with the God-given desire to find worth in and from life-giving relationships *and* a yes said to me in this condition of profound distortion.

When Hans Kung, in his epoch-making study of justification,

lines up Karl Barth's Reformed view of God's relation to the sinful creature with the Roman Catholic (especially Trent's) understanding of the same, he finds overall (not in every statement of each position) deep affinities, even agreement. For both Barth and the Catholic perspective, the human person, no matter how isolated in sin, is *never* simply graceless, for two reasons. First, creaturely existence is a constant gift offered by the Creator ever faithful to creation. Second, every human being and the entire human race as a whole are constantly being created in Jesus Christ, and are oriented to Christ as God's covenant with us, which is thoroughly God's commitment to us and for us even in our sinful state. In the unjustified, in those who have not been reborn to life in the Spirit, there is still human nature, intact with all its human capacities, still capable of freedom of choice in the most elemental sense. But there is also in the sinful, unjustified person an orientation toward covenant, given to the creature as pure gift of the self-revealing God that shows up as a quest, a hunger for something which the creature as creature and as sinner cannot possibly attain on its own, even to a minute degree: a hunger for participation in God's life and transformation of that radically sinful condition which blocks that participation. With God's acceptance, God's love as covenant partner works its way into the creature and elicits—by grace alone—that acceptance of the offer which both the Catholic and Reformed traditions call faith. Our hunger, our quest, up till now impotent but still the mark of God's gift, begins to be fulfilled, "comes home," as God begins to fulfill that orienting hunger for genuine life which was God's gracious "implant" in us from the start, and which sin, no matter how radical, could not shake off.

It is crucial to emphasize that for Barth the sinner's orientation to Christ is not due to some autonomous, *a priori* openness to God's life which the sinner possesses, but because God, all along, even while people were still sinners, was orienting them to Christ in a way that makes God's acceptance *our* most secure "possession"—purely as gift. Thus both the best of Barthian reflection and the best of the Catholic tradition maintain that, indeed, all is grace, the grace of actual acceptance by God, the grace of capacity for and the orienta-tion toward acceptance, and the grace of *our* acceptance of God's acceptance of us. All of this allows us to begin to become *someone* for God, self and others with the dignity and worth of a child in the household of God.

3 Grace as Conversion

It may initially seem strange to be treating grace as conversion only in this chapter. The reader must have recognized that there is a conversion element in the "principle and foundation" experience of acceptance. Surely, to be moved by the Lord's accepting love to a sense of one's own acceptability precisely as gift and to respond to God's acceptance with an initial, God-empowered act of acceptance of God, self and others seems to qualify as conversion experience. This is indeed true. In the theology of grace, a unitary experience is at stake, and distinctions arise for theologians because of the richness of the experience, and not in order to compartmentalize aspects that are concrete and living only when held together.

The same problem emerges in the traditional distinctions between justification and sanctification and between faith and love. The distinctions are not separations but are meant to express an internally multiple, richly living unity. The following reflection will, I hope, make it clearer why I am reserving the term conversion to this second phase of the process of Christian identity.

The acceptance dynamic I have described is, evidently, a thoroughly relational one. The accepting love offered us is offered by the God of the covenant, who is thus demonstrating his infinite love for us. The sense of lovability awakened in us is also thoroughly gift from the Other, and our response of acceptance, of an initial yes to this God, to self and to others is a movement toward the other and for the other that spells the beginning of true identity *in* ourselves by a paradox that is central to Christianity. The twin ontological dynamisms that Ernest Becker wrote of—the desire to be special and the desire to surrender to a larger, meaning-giving Whole—are put

21

back on the right track, made straight and correct ("justified") by the God who implanted those dynamisms in us human beings in the first place.

Thus the accepting love of God, working deep in the psyche and spirit, draws the falsely self-assertive and harmfully dependent ego into relationship that is life-giving. My self-love now begins to be a healthy one, fruit of the gracious offer that I am learning to accept. It is only a matter of time for this new consciousness of self, God and others to show signs of a new phase: I begin to feel hurt and sorrow. Why is that? Because the harm I was doing to myself and to the relationships that make for real life is now experienced *as* harm, because I am aware that I have been hurting the ones I love: God, self, or others. Previous to the acceptance experience I was at home with the harm, since I was hurting what I was also rejecting—my own true identity as someone for others. For many people, self-destructive tendencies can feel "natural" for years on end. Christianity maintains that the self-hating person cannot avow the real truth about the violence and sin being done to self and one's relationships. As Sebastian Moore puts it, avowal of sin in a Christian (and thus truly human) manner is possible only for the person who graciously loves self, who has, if you will, a gracious self-concept.

At this point, the violence that has been part of our "normal" way of acting can come out in the open and show itself for what it is: violence, evil, harm to the beloved creature. Sorrow, shame and confusion, healthy feelings about the self-inflicted hurt, emerge almost organically (yet as fruit of God's love and thus freely as well) when the acceptance experience puts down roots deep into the soil of the human spirit. A striking example of this is the person who, after having a genuine experience of God's love during a directed retreat, is moved by that experience to wrestle with his or her sinfulness. This movement is not the result of the retreat director's prodding, but the almost inevitable partial fruit of that initial experience. We usually cannot afford to avow our guilt for what it most basically is: not transgression of law, or failure to live up to our potential, but willful violence to self and our most essential relationships. In a climate of acceptance, the possibility of such avowal becomes concrete and inviting.

The acceptance of self, God and others that is grace-given means the beginning of a process that involves God's love drawing me from willful isolation (sin) to genuine relationship. God's love is converting me at this point. What needs conversion? *I* need conversion, at root, to be sure, but my goodness and my guilt also need conversion. Why is this so?

Often we think of ourselves as made up of two dimensions, the good and the guilty, the first non-problematic and the latter definitely problematic. Our goodness is to be preserved and fostered and the sin needs transformation. Now there is a certain common sense to this view. The surprising thing, however, is that Christianity, both Protestant and Catholic, proclaims that we in our entirety need conversion and transformation, not only because the natural in us needs to be graced, but because *all* of us is threatened by the dark power of sin. Not only our sin in the sense of our more obviously destructive side, but also the gifts, talents and experiences of yesterday, need to be drawn out of isolation or tendency toward isolation into life-giving relationship. There is a centripetal tendency in both our goodness and sins, an egoism that is an egoism of goodness and of sin. How many times do we use our goodness, our special talents, our strengths, our freedom—which really are good in themselves—as weapons against others, or bulwarks to protect us from the appeal of the less fortunate, the hungry, or the oppressed? Consider how often we hide ourselves in our sins and allow a descending spiral of internalized guilt and its external documentation (our sinful deeds) to lock us into a yet more deadly isolation. Christianity confronts us with this startling news: goodness as such isn't *the* problem, and our sins aren't the problem. Rather, the willful isolation of both our goodness and our sins is the life-or-death issue.

And so it is that the accepting, gracious God of love draws *ourselves* and *our* goodness and guilt out of isolation into companionship. This movement on God's part uncovers our intrinsic convertibility precisely as grace. Furthermore, this divine drawing of *us* empowers a responsive active conversion, by which we place ourselves, our goodness and our guilt into the new relationship with God, self and others. This responsive and active conversion blossoms into the responsive and life-giving enactment of our goodness and our guilt in thankful avowal of gifts and sorrowful confession of sins.

Our violence to ourselves which is our willful isolation becomes at this point a gracious, symbolic transformative enactment of our identity in the responsive avowal of sin and goodness which is the fruit and experience of God's conversion of us: the forgiveness of our sins and the humbling of our goodness.

Conversion and Christology

Contemporary Christology has allowed Christians to appreciate the event of Jesus Christ as an—indeed, *the*—event of grace, so that the dynamics of grace can be found in the narrative shape of Jesus' life, death and resurrection, as well as in the lives of Christians bound to Christ in faith and in the lives of all human persons as graced creatures. The dynamic I have called conversion was at work in Jesus' own relationship to the Father in the Spirit, as well as a possibility which he offered to others.[11]

In the course of Jesus' earthly life, the Father's love as radical acceptance of him was the ground of his identity. This accepting love of the Father was at the same time a converting love, in the sense that all the goodness of Jesus' humanity, all Jesus' history with the Father, with his parents and friends, all his gifts of personality, of capacity for social converse with others, all these dimensions of creaturely life, were continually drawn into the fundamental relationship of Jesus to the Father and thus were prevented from being a source of false self-assertion on Jesus' part. Jesus, empowered by this being-drawn, experienced the convertibility of his goodness and gifts, that is, their aptness for conversion, and, in a lifetime of committed freedom, actively and responsively converted or turned himself and his gifts in the direction of the Father and the Father's Kingdom. This placing of his talents, graces and being in the care of the Father and in the service of the Kingdom was empowered by the Father's drawing of Jesus. In contemporary theological language, Jesus' active transcendence toward the Father is centered in an initial, undergirding attraction of Jesus by the Holy Mystery of his life, whom he called "Abba."

The fact that Jesus' gifts and his human identity never became a tool of self-assertion to the detriment of his open availability to the Father shows itself in the room he had in his life for others and for their needs and concerns. We have already seen this room, this openness to others, in the form of acceptance offered to others. If this acceptance really became contagious, if it began to work its way into the hearts and viscera of the people Jesus touched, then a revolution could begin within them.

For the publican, the guilt-ridden, the seriously sick or bound person, this acceptance would allow a life-giving hurt, sorrow and remorse to occur, different from the dull, almost natural feeling of guilt-riddenness which knew no relief. Beginning to love himself, the publican could begin to grieve for the harm he had been doing to the (now) beloved. The vicious spiral would break open and the possibility of new life would open up. I like to think of Zaccheus as just such a person. Like most of the Synoptic narratives, the story of this curious tax collector is sharply telescoped and little attention is given to his interior journey. But the acceptance offered to him by Jesus is implicit in Jesus' request (no, command) to visit his home, and the response to this acceptance is a change of life in making recompense for his sins. The promise to right the wrong, the conversion, is not the condition for Jesus' acceptance of Zaccheus. The acceptance, unconditionally offered, unbalances this man who, because of his way of life, is no doubt deeply mired in guilt. He is able to enact his guilt, now not in a destructive way (i.e., sin) but in a life-giving, relational way, by avowing his guilt and setting it right. Jesus, or rather God through Jesus, draws Zaccheus from isolation into relationship, and, empowered by that invitation, Zaccheus actively and responsively converts.

The self-righteous types in Jesus' world were a tougher lot to work with. They didn't know they needed acceptance, and, furthermore, they didn't know they needed conversion. Jesus offered acceptance to them (he dined in their homes, for example) but he did something else as well: he promoted them to sinners, as Sebastian Moore suggests.[12] Jesus promoted them to sinners by showing, for example, how everyone is in some real way an adulterer or fornicator. Jesus' strategy here didn't consist in loading guilt onto people, but in offering acceptance and at the same time trying to make them vulnerable to God's love. The self-righteous, as such, were invulnerable to surprising grace. They had mapped their religious universe and they knew exactly where they stood. Jesus tried to pull the mat out from under them, so that they might learn to become needy for, and dependent on, grace, sheer gift. Sometimes his strategy worked, sometimes not.

In both cases, the willful isolation of one's sins or one's goodness is the spiritual problem. And in each case, Jesus draws that sin and goodness into relationship with his Father, so that the individual is able actively to confess the sin *or* the goodness to the praise of the Father. If the Pharisee becomes vulnerable to grace through his promotion to sinner, then he can bring to the Lord his gifts and good deeds in a spirit of gratitude, which is a celebration of gift and recognition that his goodness is his, but his by being sheer grace, proceeding from the Divine Other.

In the light of Easter we can see the Cross as the place where God's love is offered by Jesus to his persecutors and his betraying disciples, perhaps in muteness, perhaps in words which we find on Jesus' lips in the Gospels. On Good Friday, the responsive enactment that is going on in those who are related to Jesus is sinful rejection, either by crucifixion or by desertion. The dynamism at work is the power of sin, which, if left to itself, would destroy the human as such and so try to kill God (by killing God's image). Conversion is not occurring on Good Friday. The accepting love of Jesus has lured out into the open sin with its two faces, aggressive violence and traitorous flight. On the Cross, God's love, authentic humanity, distorted humanity, and the power of sin meet in full, unsurpassable, mutual encounter. Jesus is the tent of meeting of the human, the divine, and the dark power of sin. Jesus loves, and God loves through Jesus, humankind at its absolute worst, when humans conspire with sin as the blatant, out-in-the-open attempt at God's life through attack on God's image. This full-bodied meeting is ingredient in the total process which God is empowering: a process of conversion of humans at their most sinful. The way God chose is the most realistic, involving as it does God's full self-exposure to the world in its created goodness and bottomless guilt. Jesus is that full self-exposure. Sin comes out of hiding completely in this meeting, shows its utter violence and aggression and meets head-on God's love in its full incarnation. The power of sin, which derives from secrecy and isolation, is thus destroyed as an ultimate danger to us and to God's hopes for us.

But the story continues. The violent enactment of sin on Jesus is not yet conversion of the world. The total surrender of Jesus to the Father and his total surrender into the hands of sinners means that God's love touches people at their basest selves, accepts them and empowers change. It is the disciples who, in their Easter experience, receive the empowering word of *shalom* from the Risen One and are drawn by him into converting from traitors to disciples in a radically new way, since they are converted in their deepest potentiality to betray.[13] Of course, in the accounts as we have them now, the evangelists stress the ministry of forgiveness which the commissioned disciples are to exercise, but they are first themselves, I suggest, the recipients of Jesus' acceptance which allows them to enact their guilt, but now symbolically and healingly, in the avowal of their sin. Thus the Easter experience, foundational for the life of the Church, is an experience of acceptance and conversion, offered and received, at that point where God acts most really as God and humans enact their most violent assault against their own humanity. So founded, the Church, maintained in the truth of the Spirit, will be the place of reconciliation on which the gates of hell will have no purchase.

The Renewal of Forgiveness as Sacrament

In the New Testament, the notion of sin is sometimes considerably different from the ordinary sense of that term for most Christians. In Paul, for example, sin is more often than not spoken of in the singular, and his language is symbolic, even mythic. In Romans 5 sin is a power or reality which enters the world through one man's sin; it documents itself, so to speak, through the sins of people in the plural, but sin is not reducible simply to individual culpable transgressions, violations or faults. The mythic language for sin is employed by Paul with some sophistication, since it is clear that sin is not a substance, existing in and of itself, and equal to, or threatening to be equal to, God. Rather, the reason why mythic and not merely moralistic language has a role when giving expression to the human experience of sin is that sin shows itself to the believer as a dark, unintelligible but real possibility and power which, left to itself—in other words, not contained by a countervailing power— would destroy the human, distort creation totally, and through that total violence try to undo the very Godhead as well. The reason that sin cannot carry out this dark dynamism is that God is totally committed to creation and graces it with an ability to withstand this dark power and possibility.

Central to biblical faith is the conviction that sin emerged as a fact not with God's creation of the human, but rather came to be contingently, from the human, from men's and women's misuse of their freedom in their relation to self, God and others. Once it occurred, sin became an atmosphere and environment which almost seemed natural, "only human." For different cultures and different individuals various deeds and omissions are acknowledged as evil, but in every period of history self-centeredness and idolatry has been part of the warp and woof of the ordinary private and social world. Like the wheat and chaff of the Gospel, the sinful self-maintenance and the healthy bonds of relationship among humans are so inextricably tied together that the social cement of a cultural, economic and political world could well melt down if the sinful dimension were to be eliminated at a stroke. The naturalness and ordinariness of our guilt is due to a number of factors. First, we hide our sin, our willful and harmful self-assertion and idolatry, from ourselves, that is, from our daylight consciousness. Second, we rationalize that sinfulness of which our more explicit, conceptual consciousness is aware. Third, we find confirmation of our distorted world in the attitudes and behavior of others. What I am doing to myself and others, even if actually destructive of real life and authentic selfhood, looks familiar, and so "all right." If everyone else in the precinct takes a bribe, why shouldn't I?

Now guilt on this level of atmosphere or diffuse power (some would say, sin as "sin of the world") can do its damage unheeded for great periods of time. The deepest naturalness about this sin is due to my self-estrangement and self-hatred, which I disguise even from myself. God's love, as Moore puts it, enters into human affairs and lures the *atmosphere* into expressing itself as *act*. In the Christ event this happens in Jesus' rejection and crucifixion. God doesn't want the suffering and death of Jesus; rather God desires that creation accept the Kingdom. The effect of this offer is to empower people to change to a healthy love of self and others, as we've seen, or to enter more deeply and intransigently into their hatred of self and others. In either case, sin as atmosphere or "natural" context comes into the open as an act, either as a horrendous violation of the human, or as lovingly confessed, and so symbolically transformed, guilt.

The act of confession is crucial to the knowledge of guilt for what it is. Paul Ricoeur, in his magisterial work *The Symbolism of Evil,* insists on this.[14] Sin is not simply a disposition, or attitude, or atmosphere in its deepest essence; nor is it simply a morally reprehensible act. Sin is measured by God's own life, as the most real horizon with which sin is in conflict. It is act which hides as atmosphere and thus is most harmful because of this ability to hide. In the loving response of the accepted Christian, sin is revealed and overcome by God's love made flesh, as it were, in the confessing act. All other views of sin, which do not allow its full reality to be seen right at the point of grace's victory over it, are inadequate and misleading. Only grace reveals the true nature of sin.

In other words, faith sees an analogy between the death and resurrection of Jesus and the act of confession of sin. In each case atmosphere becomes enactment in response to God's offer of love. In each case the full reality of sin becomes manifest in its leaving its hiding place in the ordinariness of the human heart and social structures, when it meets God's love as that love draws absolutely close. The enactment in the Christ event is destructive: destructive of Jesus' earthly life, and, more terribly, destructive of the authentic humanity of the persecutors and betrayers. The Easter event continues the process of God's offer of life through Jesus as the disciples allow themselves to be transformed. They receive Christ's peace, can admit their sin and become disciples of the Risen Lord in a radically new way. In the confession of modern day Christians, when it happens with real depth, not only actions and specific omissions are signed forth, but also that dark possibility and power in them, which they conspire with in their depths to a degree they cannot have absolute clarity about. Thus, when holy persons confess, "I am the worst of sinners" they are confessing the dark possibility within themselves to reject God completely, with which they conspire and with which they would be conniving immeasurably more if it were not for God's love at work in their lives.

If we look at the revised rite of the sacrament of reconciliation in this light, we see that the rite embodies this fundamental dynamic of

Christian identity. In the case of both individual and communal celebration, the presider invites the penitent or penitents to listen first to the accepting love of God expressed in Scripture. God's word is first, and that word is the same as Jesus' word to those he invited to sup with him: "I love you just as you are." This word of love empowers and urges an initial love of God, self and others that comes to fruit in the responsive enactment of one's sin and one's gifts. Both the guilt and goodness of the past are now presented as gifts— analogous to the offertory of the Eucharistic liturgy—as they are converted into the stuff of life-giving relationship with God, self and neighbor in community.

In this perspective, the new rite teaches us the importance of confession of sin and goodness as an essential moment in a *larger* process. Confession is important not for juridical reasons primarily; the point is not that a legal condition has been fulfilled, but that a life-giving condition has been actualized. For forgiveness is not an act in which God says, in an almost magical way, "You sinned, but that's O.K." Forgiveness is a grace-empowered process of healing which is as organic in its deployment as it is sheer gift in relation to its divine Source.

When should sin be confessed to an official representative of the Church? The Catholic Church, in its early history, decreed that all public serious sins be so confessed. Later, all serious sins, as hurtful of the life of the ecclesial community, became the "matter" of the sacrament. It is clear, at any rate, that the sacramental-ecclesial celebration of the Church depends on a genuine sense that sin, even when most private, is profoundly social. Not all Christians have that sense. In order to recover it, the wisest preparation for a renewed sense of the sacrament might well consist in a more frequent experience of asking for, offering and receiving forgiveness from those persons against whom we have sinned. The sacrament of penance was never meant to lead Christians away from the practice, so difficult but so healing, of forgiving each other's sins, to which the New Testament urges us with such insistence and promise. For in this experience of offered and accepted forgiveness we experience most concretely the Father's forgiveness: Forgive us our trespasses, *as* we forgive (i.e., by embodying your forgiveness in and through our forgiveness of) those who trespass against us." God's forgiveness of us is conditional on our forgiving each other in the sense that our mutual forgiveness is the daily sacrament, the real symbol, of God's forgiveness of us: the sign which causes the grace precisely by giving full human expression to it.

Justification in a Universal Perspective

In the last chapter we saw how contemporary theologians such as Barth and Rahner respect the deep affinity between the human person and community and God's grace on the one hand, and the sheer gift character of that grace on the other. God's self-communication is more than the creature can ever become or bring about. Certainly it is more than the creature can earn or be equal to, because God is sharing with creatures the very divine being and life. On the other hand, we are able to become fully human only to the extent that we live open to and receptive of this infinite gift. Barth calls this relation between the creature and God's grace "creation in Jesus Christ" and Rahner names it "the supernatural existential." Even in our rejection of God's love, we continue to receive a positive orientation to that love, in such wise that our sin is a contradiction of our being in its deepest, most concrete nature. This grace of "creation in Christ" or "supernatural existential" cannot be lost; we cannot shake ourselves loose from it, so to speak. We are graced to be this way—always. Thus God's accepting love is extended to a creature whom God has already oriented to that acceptance. What we most need in life is gift and this is our constant need. That is the paradox which Christianity discloses in its full dimension but which every person who has experienced human love has glimpsed.

In this chapter we have been looking at the continuation of the acceptance process in the form of conversion: forgiveness of sin and grateful avowal of goodness. Taken together, acceptance and conversion are traditionally called justification. In this process we are made "just" before God and in relation to God and God's creation. In other words, we are made friends of God from being enemies, children of the household of God from being slaves and strangers.

In traditional Catholic theology, justification comes to the individual either through sacramental baptism or baptism of desire or blood. The former can, of course, occur in the life of an infant or adult, the latter two forms only in someone who is capable of responsible decision. In reinterpreting the Christian understanding of justification, Karl Rahner does not simply repeat the earlier understanding but tries to penetrate to the central truth of the doctrine which allows him to modify its less central aspects. For Rahner, justification is God's forgiving and divinizing love as freely accepted grace, accepted, that is, by humankind. In the mode of offer only, grace is not justifying, because it has not yet become historical; it is not yet affecting the human in its own freedom. When does God's offered grace become offered *and* accepted? In Rahner's understanding, this occurs when the full offer is received completely through the entirety of a human life unto death (i.e., unto completion of that life). Now Jesus of Nazareth is the one person in whom God's self-offer is totally and freely accepted. He participated fully in the divine life and all his human life was constantly drawn into obedient relationship to the Father and compassionate identification with sinners. This is the very grace which God wants to give to all God's creation. To be sure, there was offer and acceptance in salvation history prior to Jesus' emergence in the world. But the acceptance was never total; it was always sin-tainted and fragmentary. As Rahner puts it, in Jesus' life, death and resurrection, we have the beginning of the absolute, irreversible and unsurpassable history of God's self-communication and its total acceptance. This saving self-communication encompasses all people and all history, since it all along is being offered *to* history as well as in and through it.

The Church is the sacrament of this victorious grace of Christ. For Rahner, the Church does not provide boundaries for grace, but rather is the effective *sign* of grace's universal presence in all of history, implicitly or explicitly known by people. The Church then is the continuation of Jesus' presence in history in his victory over sin and death. It is by virtue of the presence of Christ in history, first in Palestine and then ecclesially, that God's justifying grace is in the world as offer and acceptance. God's offer is accepted by Jesus and the Church as the Body of Christ in the Spirit. In its fullest expression within history, justification occurs as sacramental baptism. Yet justification is not restricted to baptism, but is a universal possibility. Rahner's reflections at this point involve several steps.

Every human person is born into a redeemed history that is still a broken sinful history. These are not two, juxtaposed, equally potent factors in the person's life. Rather, the redemption of the world in Christ is more powerful than the power of sin, but its victory is not yet eschatologically complete. Thus everyone is born in Christ and in "Adam" (as symbol of broken humanity). The former dimension or existential might be termed original redemptive grace, since it is redemptive grace that is offered to each person at the origin of each human life, chronologically and existentially. The latter dynamic is original sin, meaning the sin of humankind from its origin which affects us from the beginning of our lives and at root. If left to itself, original sin would take over the entire person to his or her destruction. But, in the concrete, there has never been, nor will there ever be, a purely graceless person, thanks to God's fidelity to the creation God has oriented to sharing the divine life.

Born with these two real, yet unequal existentials, a child is not yet justified. To be sure, God is offering justifying grace in Christ to the child in its spiritual depths, but that offer is actually justifying only if it comes to effective expression in a communitarian way. Justification is right relationship toward God and God's created world, particularly the human community. The righting of the relationship with the community is the expressive cause (sacrament) of the actual, effective justification before God, so closely does God bind union with God and union with creatures. But in the case of the child who is not baptized—the vast majority of children born into human history—how are they justified? Rahner suggests that any gesture of acceptance of the child into the (redeemed) human family can be appreciated as the sign of justifying grace, effective *ex opere operato,* i.e., effective by virtue of Christ's victorious grace. Thus in analogy with baptism, which happens to a child contingently as initiation into the family of the Church, such a gesture, in all its simplicity and contingency, is bearer of God's accepting and converting love. For the non-Christian this acceptance of the child is laden with all the human (including religious) meaning that is intended by the one accepting, but it is also, thanks to Christ's grace universally present in the world through the Church, the justification of the child.[15]

Justified, the person continues to have two existentials (orientation to God in Christ and orientation to "Adam"). But the crucial difference is that the one orientation has been transformed into a participation in Christ's and the Church's acceptance of the orientation, while the second orientation is present only as the effects of the "road not taken": traditionally, concupiscence as weakness of heart, mind and will regarding the moral good, and death as a dark and threatening peril in our lives.

Furthermore, the presence of offered and (ecclesially) accepted grace in the child is dynamically oriented to becoming grace in the mode of *personal* acceptance. In fact, Rahner and most other contemporary Roman Catholic theologians view adult faith, adult justification and adult relationship to God, Christ and Church as the primary form of grace, in the light of which the limit case of infant participation in faith, justification and relation to Christ and Church should be interpreted. For grace has "come home," has become its full reality, only when it becomes fully and freely accepted by the person and community, supported and empowered by God's full and free offer of God's self.

4 Grace as Discipleship in Community

It is only at this point in our reflections that relationship to Jesus Christ and the Church becomes our theme, even though Christ and the Church are what is most "Christian" about Christian experience. All along, the living context in which acceptance and conversion of goodness and guilt were occurring was the Church and the relationship to Christ which is the heart of the Church. But often, when a breakthrough occurs in the first two places, then Christians are able to experience—*afresh*—the realities of discipleship and community.

That the explicit starting point of Christian existence need not be either Christ or the Church comes home to the thoughtful reader of Karl Rahner's masterful *Foundations of Christian Faith*. Rahner presents here a first level of reflection on the meaningfulness and truth of Christian faith for people of today. His audience is first of all Christians, indeed Catholic Christians, but he hopes to make sense to other Christians and non-Christians as well. By means of this first level of reflection, Rahner tries to disclose the inner affinity between our human experience and the Christian message of salvation, as well as the gift-character of that message. Rahner begins his book with a consideration of the human person and human community as hearers of the message, as open to and oriented to the Absolute Mystery we call God, and as threatened by guilt and experiencing forgiveness. Only then does he treat—and at great length—the mystery of Jesus Christ, the Church and Christian existence in the world. This sequence is not simply pedagogical; it reflects the development of our consciousness of grace. All of Rahner's theology, documented in over fifty years of writing, attests that he is a theologian of grace *par excellence*. From beginning to end of *Foundations* he is exploring the experience of grace as human (social and individual), Christological and ecclesial. Encounter with Jesus Christ is the explicit expression of what humans experience in all the depth and breadth of their lives: the self-communication of God as the ultimate and most intimate horizon of all human life.

This perspective can be clarified by consideration of Christian religious experience. Sebastian Moore agrees with Rahner when he writes that the experience in faith of the real Jesus Christ—really human and thoroughly divine—is possible only under certain conditions. Many individuals or communities have a genuine meeting with the real Christ, as distinct from an idealized or mythological entity, only if the person or group has experienced a breakthrough in their sense of their own concrete humanity as touched by the love of the real God. In the context of such meeting, we are empowered, as we have seen, to accept the real God into our lives and to accept our real humanity on God's terms. This leads to the conversion process by which we are drawn from isolation into relationship; our goodness and our guilt are humbled, that is, drawn into life-giving relationship with God.

But this real (as distinct from thought-about) union of our real selves and the real God is precisely the context in which we can know Jesus Christ in personal relationship. This is because Jesus is *the* graced one, *the* Man of grace, who is the full union of authentic humanness and real (not "ideal") divinity. Thanks to the dynamics of grace up until this point, we have access to Jesus, experientially (not just as a matter of "up-to-date" Christology), as one of us and one with God. Until this point, we are torn between an idealized view of our humanness (euphoria) which makes it into something very unreal, and a rejection of and estrangement from our real, broken humanity (depression). In addition, we swing between two unreal views of God: as rejecting us in our guilt, *or* as rival to or prolongation of our self-assertiveness.

But now, at this new stage, the New Testament narratives come alive. Now, as loved sinners, we can appreciate with our hearts and minds that God in Christ wants to be with sinners, that authentic humanity does not mean the removal of Jesus into some isolated, superior status, but rather his freedom to be with sinners, and his cherishing of that companionship. This acceptance and conversion work a psychological and spiritual revolution in us, so that we discover Jesus in a wholly new way. This breakthrough experience can be dramatic or gentle; it can be repeated, on new levels, many times in our lives, but each time it is an accepting and converting love which brings us to him.

This point is documented many times over when people come to recognize why for so long they had trouble with the humanity of Jesus. Their difficulty may be due to poor education, but this misfortune only feeds the deeper problem. And the deeper problem is our brokenness, our rejection of our own authentic, God-given humanity and our willful perception of God as the arch-rival of our ego and its drive to be the center of things. When the healing of our God-concept and self-concept is worked in us by God's grace, then there is room in our psyches and spirits for the real Jesus Christ, the union of real humanness and the real God.

Discipleship is nothing else than the personal, intimate relationship with Christ by which we learn in practical, life-changing ways who God is for us and who we are called to be. Discipleship is initiation into Jesus' relationship with the Father and into his relationships with other people. It is the learning of his strategy regarding the Kingdom; it is discovering with Jesus how to pray and how to act, how to assume responsibility and how to become responsive, how to suffer and how to die. Grace now becomes grace with a countenance, grace with a name. We discover Jesus in a new way, and yet the discovery is a recognition of him who was implicitly at work in us up until now, accepting us and leading us into the life-giving conversion of our goodness and guilt.

Edward Schillebeeckx's massive work on grace in the New Testament supports this viewpoint as well.[16] Throughout his study, the fundamental experience which shapes the early Church is the gift of salvation from God: forgiveness of sin and participation in God's life, as liberation and promise of fulfillment for humanity. Within this primary experience, Jesus of Nazareth is known and proclaimed as the one in and through whom that salvation is given to our world. Schillebeeckx even calls Christology, in the sense of the second

article of the Creed, "concentrated creation" because it enunciates
God's fidelity both to creation and to the divine passion to give God
to us for our humanization that comes to full expressive enactment in
Christ.[17] Another way he expresses this is to say that soteriology, an
experience of God's Kingdom as human salvation, precedes
Christology—the sense of Christ's identity.

> Even the unique Easter experience is a soteriological event.
> Only then does the question "Who is he who is able to
> accomplish such things?" take on full significance. In other
> words, to adopt a modern Jewish distinction, explicit
> "who-religion" follows after "what-religion"; for the "who-
> christology" is already implicit in the "what-christology."
> From this point of view, the soteriological question of
> christology is in fact a "second-order" question, because it
> already presupposes a first event, the experience of
> salvation with Jesus.[18]

The encounter with Jesus is not a private one, however. The
process of Christian identity as a story of grace means that we find
ourselves joined with others in a discipleship relation with Christ.
The bond which unites us is the experience of acceptance and
forgiveness which draws our humbled goodness and forgiven guilt,
all that we are, into relationship with God who leads us to Christ. The
stuff of discipleship is the same as the "building-blocks" of our
community: our converted goodness and guilt drawn by God into
relationship with Christ and others. Reconciliation is the way that
community is fashioned, and not simply an occasional "remedy" for
an otherwise healthy communal experience. We are loved sinners
and, having experienced ourselves as such, can be at home with the
real Christ *and* in the real graced and broken Church of sinners. The
grace of conversion becomes personal in Christ and social in the
Church—all of it gift, all of it life-giving process.

Jesus' Fellowship with God and Sinners

Discipleship first fashions Jesus' own identity before it becomes a relationship into which Jesus calls people. The narratives of both the Synoptic and Johannine Gospels express the identity of Jesus as one who gains all from the Father, one who learns all from the Father. Just as a son is initiated into a craft, indeed a whole life-style, by his father, so Jesus has been instructed by contemplating what his Father does. Jesus is essentially learner, and his Father the primary teacher. To be sure, Mary and Joseph and the other significant adults in Jesus' life touched and shaped his human mind, heart and imagination. But there is an unfathomable aloneness in Jesus' relation to the Father that is not a matter of human mediation but a relationship of giving and receiving that is between Jesus and the Holy Mystery whom he addressed as "Abba." There was no "Moses" for Jesus, no fellow human who was the fully adequate mediator between Jesus and God. We, as Christians, do have such a mediator; but Jesus, precisely in this dimension of his life, differs from us. It is well-nigh impossible to get positive insight into this difference, for it is a solitude that he could only indirectly indicate through the way he addressed God and the ways in which he proclaimed the Kingdom in word and deed.

Just as Jesus was primarily disciple of the Father, so his primary attitude was that of obedience. The Jesus of the earthly ministry as he is witnessed to in the Gospels is the one who is joyfully subordinate to the Father as divine center of his life. He is one who says no more than he has heard. In Paul, obedience is the word that characterizes Jesus' stance vis-a-vis the Father, especially, indeed consummately, on the cross. Jesus' free obedience is at once a responsive listening to God (*ob-audire*) and a free subjection to the powers of sin even though by rights he was free of sin and death, being the perfect image of God (cf Phil 2:6-11).

Jesus' primary community is with the Father. It is a relationship of shared life, understanding and will which transcends the community of his Israelite people, even though Jesus was deeply one of his people, a Jew among Jews. Jesus' communion in prayer and obedient acting and suffering is the human form of his responsive identity in relation to the Father.

As disciple of the Father and one who stands in deepest *koinonia* (fellowship) with the Father, Jesus is able to draw others into discipleship and community in a wholly new way. Martin

Hengel, in a monograph on Jesus' manner of calling people into discipleship, indicates the remarkable character of Jesus' claim on people.[19] Jesus takes the initiative, unlike the rabbis who would rather be approached by would-be students and asked to admit them to discipleship. Jesus, in a saying which Hengel takes to be authentic, invites a man to join with him in proclaiming the nearness of the Kingdom. The man appeals to sacred taboo and the fourth commandment when he expresses his desire to bury his father first. Indeed, this obligation was one which the rabbis permitted even if it meant non-observance of the Law. But Jesus says to him, "Let the dead bury their dead." That is, let those dead to the nearness of the Kingdom take care of such secondary obligations. The grace of discipleship is a call, claim and empowerment which comes from Jesus and challenges the recipient to respond with equal wholeheartedness. Jesus lays claim on this man precisely the way Yahweh laid claim on the prophets in the Old Testament.

The *koinonia* which Jesus experienced with the Father empowered Jesus to draw people into deeper community with their God and each other in relation to Jesus. In calling the disciples, Jesus laid claim on them and bound them to himself and to the Kingdom he preached. His call was the link which united them. Furthermore, as we have seen, Jesus was concerned in his ministry with the excommunicates, the demoniacs, the seriously ill, and public sinners like prostitutes and tax collectors. He did not lead these people away from the community of Israel, but restored them to it, while renewing that community. In a number of the exorcisms and healings, the person is returned to the ordinary life of the people, where, for the Jew, grace and salvation were to be found.

It is on the cross that Jesus' oneness with God in discipleship and communion and his fellowship with the excommunicates become total. The former relationship becomes totally hidden, even, it would seem, for Jesus. The latter form of solidarity becomes murderously apparent. Jesus dies a violent, degrading, dehumanizing death. He is subjected to a form of execution which tries to expel those so executed from the human family, and, in this case, from the Israelite community of salvation. Outside the city, on a garbage dump, he dies, displayed as a non-person, a slave. The identification with excommunicates is complete. The Father's relationship to Jesus silently and hiddenly sustains Jesus, giving him his only support. His communion with the Father, which he experiences now only in blind trust, grounds the fact that there is no place in Jesus where he is superior to or exclusive of his executioners or the disciples who are betraying him. They, in their sinning, get to him completely. Paul has a shocking word for it: "God made him sin who knew no sin" (2 Cor 5:21). He becomes the body, the form, of their sinning; he displays in his being the true nature of their sin and all sin's violent assault on the authentically human and, through that, on God. Jesus doesn't die with a superior, clear conscience like a "martyr" or hero, but experiences fully the effect and power of sin: isolation from God in complete, freely accepted oneness with sinners. This is the culmination, and not merely the consequence, of Jesus' provocative ministry. He is for sinners as one of them, but out of obedience to the Father and love for them, not out of any sinning of his own.

The cross is the hour of the grace of fellowship par excellence, the hour when God's love in human form absorbs the full, publicly enacted power of sin and disarms it by refusing to play sin's game. God renounces all power-prerogatives that scare and incite the sinful ego, at a depth which strips sin of its false power. For as we have seen, sin is effective only in hiding, only apart from God's gracious love. Now is the hour of meeting between sin's fake power, played out totally, and authentic humanity, meeting and taking in all that fake power and able to do so because grounded solely in the real God, whose power bears the name of self-emptying love.

This encounter occurs on the Cross, and this is the absolutely vital condition for the victorious transformation of sinful body into body of grace. The grace of Easter consists in the full communication to the crucified Jesus of the divine life, the full return to Jesus of his fully surrendered identity, and Jesus' forgiving and divinizing offer to, and acceptance by, the traitorous disciples. In their Spirit-empowered acceptance of Jesus' acceptance and forgiveness, they are led into a radically new form of discipleship and community founded on the paschal event. They are called to be the Church of Jesus Christ, in the power of the Spirit. They become the earthly but Spirit-filled body of the Risen One, enacting in thanksgiving, table fellowship and mutual service their response to the gracious presence of the Crucified and Risen One in their midst. The discipleship and community they experience with Christ stands in deep continuity with their pre-Easter experience, but it is also something radically new. The newness derives from the saving truth that sin has been fully encountered in history and defused for all time as an ultimate, potentially victorious power over the human family. Jesus' Spirit creates the new humanity, a family shaped by faith, love and hope, and summoned to ministry to Word and sacrament. Here in the paschal event is documented for all time that God's grace is given *to* history and works itself out *in* and *through* history, for our sakes and God's glory.

The Dynamics of Discipleship in Liturgy and Personal Prayer

The graced identity of the Church is expressed most explicitly in its public worship. The living, active language of worship, not the reflex language of theology, best conveys the community's experience of the grace of Christ's presence in the Spirit which shapes the community's identity. Scripture scholars have shown that even in the New Testament the several places in which Jesus is undisputably named "God" occur in texts which are liturgical or express a liturgical situation.[20] The bold, more-than-logical language of worship was the earliest way the community expressed its experience of Christ as *God's* graciousness toward it. The language employed here is interactive and performative, evoked by and responsive to the presence of Christ as the presence of God. The primary communal language of grace is, therefore, the language of actually enacted worship; the actual singing and praying, the ritual acting, the engaged silence, all convey the meaning of the reality encountered and the reality of the Church as respondent to the presence of Christ in the encounter. The entitling of Jesus, the use of self-involving metaphors (e.g., "Our Lord") and proclamatory narrative, the movement and action of blessing and distributing convey in their boldness the point of Jesus' resurrection as the offer of gracious presence to which the community, gathered in the Spirit, answers. The presence of sacramental grace in the liturgy is not the presence of a spiritual or supernatural "something" but the personal presence of Christ in the Spirit which provokes this responsive action. Thus this action cannot be "explained" adequately by analyzing the logic of the concepts used or by analyzing the gestures and prayers in their objectifiable content. Grace is best expressed by the living dynamism of response and not in an object-like way. The grace of Christ's presence cannot be grasped in itself; it can, however, be expressed in the movement of total surrender which alone, over the span of a lifetime, "measures" up to the wholeness of the Grace being offered: Christ alive and instituting a community alive in his Spirit to the glory and praise of the Father.[21]

If we look for a moment at the fundamental dynamism of the Eucharistic liturgy in its sequence of phases, we can appreciate how that dynamism is nothing less than the grace of Christian identity, expressed and enacted communally, in the "official" sacramental self-identification of the Church as worshiping community. After the preliminary moments of greeting and reconciliation, which are designed to foster a receptive spirit in the gathering, the first major moment is the proclaiming of God's Word as word of love, principally through the Gospel but supported and given context by Old Testament and/or other parts of the New Testament. "Be silent and hear how I love you" seems to be the point here. The word of love draws and empowers the community forward into the second phase, the presentation of the gifts. Here the bread and wine and the action of presentation express performatively the community's willingness to let its life, its goodness and brokenness, be drawn forward so that they can be transformed from isolation into consecrated relationship. This is accomplished in the Eucharistic prayer, said over the gifts and the people. The change in the gifts and the assembly, wrought by the Spirit, makes possible a new actualization of community in Christ which is accomplished and expressed in Communion. The prayer after Communion and the "dismissal" give expression to the witness and service dimension of the Eucharistic assembly as people move beyond the liturgy of the Eucharist to the liturgy of daily Christian living. Acceptance, conversion, community in discipleship, witness and service: the pattern of grace in Christian life is identically the pattern of sacramental grace in the Eucharistic action of the whole assembly gathered in the Spirit in response to Christ's prompting. The grace of the sacrament is dynamic, future-oriented and hope-giving; at the same time it is inclusive of the community's past and present and transformative of them through the presiding power of Christ in the Spirit. It thus has all the earmarks of the resurrection as the central enactment and expression of God's victorious grace in Christ!

In personal prayer we can observe a similar pattern of grace. Very often prayer is called a dialogue between God and an individual. Now dialogue ordinarily involves the give and take of verbal communication, as well as the possibility of shared, communicative silences. Yet in prayer, while we often say or think words toward God, God does not, usually, speak words to the pray-ers. In what way does God ordinarily speak to the person to prayer? Karl Rahner answers this question in a simple way.[22] God "speaks" not many words but one basic word: the word divinely spoken is nothing less than the life of the one who prays, that life as constantly, lovingly created and constantly offered the self-communication of the creating God. I am the one who is "spoken." To enter into my life as one creatively oriented to God and receptive of God's life is to pray. Listening to God means listening to my life as a life being drawn into God all the time. In and through that graced openness-unto-God, I am listening to God. In Rahnerian language, the "wordless word" that I am as one spoken by God is equivalent to my graced transcendentality as such. In other words, my graced self as pre-conceptual yet conscious orientation toward God (because God is thus creating me always) is the privileged place of meeting with God. I am impeded in this listening when I look at, stay with or listen to myself or part of myself apart from this transcendence, this being drawn to God. Then I am stuck in myself, not truly praying. I am equally impeded if I leave outside of my orientation toward God some crucial part of myself (a memory, a hurt, a desire, a feeling) which I suppress or repress. Thus I am blocked in my ability to be in tune with my graced transcendence toward God.

In prayer God is accepting all that I am and have been, drawing it — the goodness and guilt — to the divine life, asking only that I conspire with this being-drawn, this transcendence. If I allow my concrete cares, concerns, desires and affections to be accepted by God, and by myself, I shall be converted into further relationship with God, self and others in deepening discipleship and community. Then my gifts and guilt—both transformed—can be the stuff of hope: of witness and service. Now the "word" of my life spoken by

God is allowed to draw into itself the many words which are the concrete details of my life history.

Rahner takes the same helpful approach in speaking of discernment.[23] Discerning God's will for me essentially consists in learning, through the discipline of love, to hear well the one word of the Lord which is my graced transcendence. I then learn how to place other, more particular choices within the field of this experienced "word" of transcendence. I discover how each particular choice, experimentally entered into, affects the basic grace-experience of openness toward the Lord. Using the language of St. Ignatius, Rahner calls the primal word "consolation without preceding cause," or consolation without an object, because this fundamental consolation is experienced as openness to the divine goal of our lives. Only God can open a creature to God's infinite life; so God's primary will for us is disclosed in this fundamental experience of orientation to God as such. We recognize God's more concrete will for us in particular circumstances by employing this fundamental consolation as the experiential grace-criterion for the other choices. It is clear why Rahner views discernment as a lifelong initiation into a primary skill of discipleship, and not as something we can automatically perform at a moment's notice.

The grace of discipleship in community is experiential, not as a particular item or object in our field of conscious experience, but as the enveloping and grounding dynamism of our whole selves (our "spirit") as oriented toward God's own life. Growth in discernment is growth in participation in Jesus Christ's own strategy for the Kingdom, for Jesus was and is *the* discerner of Abba's will, and we are given a share in *his* gift, thanks to the Spirit.

The Church: Charism and Institution

A moment ago I referred to the Eucharist as the situation in which the Church manifests its reality with a certain fullness. Discipleship in community embodies itself in a special way whenever the community gathers together for worship. In one respect, the Christians so assembled are doing the same thing which has been done since the very beginnings of the Church. The pattern of liturgy today, for all its changes down through the ages, is in real continuity with the past. Christ's command "Do this in memory of me" is a call to repeat, again and again, what he did at the Last Supper. Thus, in the sociological sense, the liturgy is a prime example of institution in the life of the Church: each liturgy is a pattern of prayers, readings and gestures which are the regulated way of celebrating the Eucharist. Catholic Christians believe that Christ has committed himself and his Spirit to the Eucharistic action of the Church. The Eucharist (with the other sacraments) is the expression which Christ's love for the Church gives itself. Thus Christ is present in the Eucharist not because of the virtuous lives of those assembled, whether the priest or the rest of the people, but by his own resurrected life, which is, in and of itself, presence to the Church. To speak of the *ex opere operato* efficacy of the sacraments is simply to put into technical language this truth of faith concerning the sacraments. They are Christ-instituted signs of his resurrected presence.

Here we have a privileged example of the union of structure and grace, institution and Spirit. The institutional makes available in repeatable fashion what ultimately is unique, totally gratuitous and in excess, as it were, of the confines of the structure: God's self-communication in Christ and his Spirit.

But there is another dimension of sacramental life in addition to God's self-communication and the repeatable structures involved in each sacrament. There is the dimension of charism, a dimension which can be transitory or permanent. If we stay with our example of the Eucharist, an instance of transitory charism would be the congregation's experience of a Spirit-filled homily offered by the celebrant. Now a charism is not a talent or natural gift, of eloquence, for example, but rather an event, the gracious activity of God through a person. This divine activity does not depend on the holiness of the individual, but has a transcendent otherness about it. Through the preacher, who at the time was eloquent or not, strong or weak, showing his closeness or distance to God, God's Spirit manifested itself to the congregation in a way, for example, which built up their faith. The charism was unpredictable, unforeseeable; it was a transitory, unrepeatable experience. The preacher exercises the charism to the extent that he remains open to God dependent on God's action. The latter, in turn, will make use of human instruments, such as the preacher's voice and speaking ability, but it does not show itself by heightening, developing or transforming a human capacity or ability.

This transitory experience of grace, however, is rooted in a more permanent charism, that of office. The preacher is endowed with grace by virtue of a public role as someone commissioned by the Church for this task. Just as Christ commits himself to the sacraments, so too he unites himself with office-holders in the Church that they might be equipped with all that is needed by way of grace for their roles. Not that charism of office develops or transforms their natural abilities, but the charism, if relied on in faith, assures that their service of the Church will be for the building up of faith, love and hope and not simply an exercise of human talent for its own sake.

So we see that God's gracious self-commitment to the Church involves both institution and charisms. Grace requires both in the pilgrim time before grace becomes final glory. And we can add with Avery Dulles that in the pilgrim Church the institutional lives off the charismatic and the charismatic off the institutional, in order that both might aid the coming of the Kingdom, when institutions and charisms will be no longer necessary.[24]

5 Grace as Witness and Service

In the process I have been describing as the dynamic of Christian identity, we have seen how God's unconditional acceptance of people can lead to an experience of forgiveness, of conversion, of goodness and guilt into relationship with God and others in Christ, which is the stuff of discipleship in community. All along this graced dynamic is fostering another dimension which needs to be accorded some particular attention. From the acceptance, through the conversion and into the community and discipleship experience there starts to emerge a healthy self-forgetfulness which allows the person or community which has let this process occur to begin to transcend themselves in attitudes and deeds of acceptance, forgiveness and love which foster communty. This self-transcendence toward the neighbor, which can occur in the graced individual or the graced group, I would prefer to express by two fundamental terms: witness and service.

Frans Jozef van Beeck has described witness well in his recent work on Christology.[25] As a witness I convey personally that I have been "touched" by Jesus Christ; my speaking and acting re-present to people Jesus Christ alive and present. The new life effected in me by Christ is conveyed to others by my actual living in praise of the source of that new life. The people to whom I witness will have to respond, either by openness or rejection, for witness places people in a decision-situation. And the decision will have to do with the witnessing person, the reality re-presented by the witness and the very person of those witnessed to. Something new arises in the decision-situation which is more than the past background of the decision. Ultimately, in and through witnessing, the very identity of the witness and the reality of the source of that identity are being offered to others in the mode of invitation, which can be either challenging or comforting depending on the circumstances.

Service is meant to refer to all the particular beneficial effects my loving actions can have on others, or which they can offer to me. Service includes all efforts to help the neighbor, whether an individual or a group, either doing for them what they cannot do for themselves or helping them come to the point where they are able to provide for themselves and in turn extend help to others. Service can be personal and societal; it can be on the level of the development or redistribution of external goods and material welfare, on the level of helping persons or communities mature in their responsibility for themselves and others, or on the level of forgiveness of sin and sharing in divine life.

Christian service involves witness as well, if the point of the service is both to help people materially and psychologically and to make known to them the reality of Christ, in new ways or for the first time. Sometimes, in extreme circumstances, service in the sense of particular beneficial actions on behalf of others must yield to witness alone, because one is incapable of service in the sense described. Jesus' life, death and resurrection offer a striking example of service rooted in witness and witness stripped of service. And both are grace.

Jesus as Witness and Servant

The primary grace-event for Christianity is the death, resurrection and incarnation of the Son of God. As we saw in the earlier chapters, there is an intimate unity between the gift-event as the self-communication of God's life and the expression and presence of that event in and through the humanity of Jesus as he lived before God and before his fellow humans. The death, resurrection and incarnation of God's Son causes this grace and salvation for us precisely the way sacrament causes grace and salvation: by expressing it, symbolizing it, rendering it a here-and-now event. "Sacramenta causant gratiam significando": sacraments cause grace by signifying it. Jesus' life and ministry, his death and his resurrection were thus witness to God's gift and service of others through that gift.[26] As narrated in the Gospels, Jesus' mission was one of both witness and service. The very boldness of his proclamation and deeds conveyed a revolutionary sense to people of the God ("Abba") who stood behind Jesus and whom Jesus represented to them. Who God *really* is, and what the reign of God is like in human and gracious terms: this Jesus communicated by what he said, but also by the way he said it, by the rhetoric (in the best sense of the word) of his actions and speech. The *exousia,* the power, the authoritativeness of his manner of speaking and doing, exceeded the particular content which was said and done. The grace-event of Jesus for those people was conveyed to them by that life-giving power which no logical analysis of the concepts and propositions he employed could ever adequately disclose. The God whose absolutely close and gracious presence in Jesus' life prompted and empowered his manner of speech and deed "came through" to people. They responded either by closure, by welcome, or by categorizing him as possessed, as drawing his power from a dark source. But no matter what the response was, in his own person Jesus was witness to God and God's reign, and witness to faith understood as openness to that God and reign. In and through Jesus' total surrender to "Abba" and God's reign, Abba's presence was communicated persuasively to others. Jesus was thus engaged in witness to God as a primary dimension of his life and activity.

But that is not all. In Jesus' self-presentation to others during his travels, as he taught and healed and exorcised, he witnessed and represented to others God's creation as God would have it be. Without calling attention to himself, but rather focusing on God and God's reign *and* on the needs of those he encountered, Jesus held up to all creation the image of its authentic, gentle, relational wholeness. "Why do you call me good? No one is good but God alone" (Mk 10:18), he said, not self-deprecatingly but in full recognition of who is good simply. He conveyed to people the true measure of creation when it is grounded in the creating and self-communicating God of the Kingdom. By parable and healing touch, by the boldness of his encounter with people as that encounter was rooted in his constant meeting with God, he witnessed to the wholeness of creation that can only come to it as pure gift. The new Adam held up to people all that they were destined for.

But as opposition and rejection increased, Jesus' witness took on another dimension. Meeting the rejection and its sinful source head-on in loving self-presentation, Jesus represented in himself the false, broken and destructive self of the one engaged in rejecting him. Absorbing the rejection into himself, he neither openly retaliated, nor responded in a subtle passive-aggressive way, nor did he secretly harden himself by excluding the rejection and its source in the other person from communion with his life and love. He bore in the freedom of his love the destructiveness of the other in a relationship to that other that was full-bodied presence.[27]

The Cross is the symbol or full actualizing expression of that total relationship of Jesus to the sinner (crucifier or traitorous disciple). Here Jesus' witness-identity becomes complete while *apparently* most powerless. On the Cross Jesus witnessed, by his full presence in love, to God's complete joining with humankind in all that it is, even as sinful. He witnessed in his own body to the sinner as the destructive one who is only really destroying self. He witnessed as well to the authentic humanity that God was offering as real possibility and gift to human beings, even while they enacted their very worst at Jesus' expense. The relational being of Jesus in full encounter with the silent, self-communicating God and with the savagery of sin, which would— if it could —dehumanize the human, is the culmination of his witness. He is, on the Cross, the totally representative one, the "tent of meeting" of God's love risking all, of sinners attempting their deadliest all, and of authentic humanity's constancy of loving identification with both God and sinners.

The witness bears a harvest, though, as Christ, in the power of the Spirit, witnesses beyond death's hold to the disciples and empowers their joyful response of acceptance, conversion, discipleship and mission. In the glory of God, the Risen One witnesses victoriously to God, to himself and to the new humanity which God in the Spirit has wrought. The Risen One offers both God's life and a transformed humanity to the sinful disciples, who are empowered and persuaded to be converted and to surrender to the Resurrected One in eschatological faith, love and hope. Now they, in turn, will become witnesses to God's definitive witness, Jesus Christ, and servants and friends of the Servant through the power and persuasion of their own lives of faith in the Spirit.

The grace of witness is conjoined in Jesus with the grace of service. Jesus in his life engaged in particular, transient deeds of service. He fed the hungry with food and God's word, he healed the sick and possessed, he challenged unjust social structures (people's shared assumptions) through parables of word and deed. There was plenty of room in Jesus' life for such provisional, limited service of people and the structures which bound them together. On the Cross service in this particular way was consummated in witness. Jesus was himself for God and sinners. In the Easter event Jesus is powerfully present to the nascent Church in the Spirit who, as Acts tells us, continued the healing, challenging and transforming work of the earthly Jesus.

The uncanny thing is this: each time the service is gift and not bondage. The gift begets gratitude, not an infinite debt which people can never pay off, and which keeps them indentured for life. The grace of Christ does not lord it over its recipients but empowers them to be themselves and to be free enough to serve others joyfully and spontaneously in turn. Real grace begets graciousness and not repayment on the installment plan. Jesus Christ, the true servant of all, neither substitutes for nor displaces anyone, but rather mysteriously opens up space for free people to present themselves in compassionate service to others, in turn not displacing but enabling those others. Not "charity" in its dependency-creating forms, but compassionate empowerment is the mark of this service and ministry. If gentleness, patience, joyfulness, spontaneity, thankfulness, and freedom are not the marks of the ones who have been served by Christ, then the message and the medium are still divorced, and the style proper to Christ's grace is still hidden from a world thirsty for it.

Performative Faith, Love, Hope

In the traditional treatises on grace, the accent fell on the habitual grace which sanctifies the soul and which renders it capable of meritorious acts of faith, hope and love. This sanctifying grace was like a second nature given to the created spiritual nature of men and women, elevating the soul to being a principle of supernatural activities. This language of nature and operations is Aristotelian, and Thomas Aquinas' use of this conceptuality was revolutionary in his day. For the medieval Christian, use of Aristotle's basic metaphysical categories served to emphasize the profound *reality* of the life of grace. This legacy has much to offer modern Christians so long as they are able to appropriate the Christianized Aristotelianism. The problem for us, however, is that even if understood within their own historical context, the most basic insights of Aquinas still require a radical reinterpretation. His emphasis on nature and operations needs to be reinterpreted in terms of intrapersonal, interpersonal and societal *relationships*. His ontic way of thinking, which illuminates the reality of persons as objective beings, needs to yield to a more adequate appreciation of grace as conscious experience of God, self and society.

Having said this, still the Christian life *is* a life of faith, love and hope. Indeed, in recent years, philosophers and theologians have given fresh attention to moral habits and moral character, and to the activities which are truly expressive of Christian identity. I have reserved mention of these three "theological" (God-oriented) virtues until now, not because they have no place in the previous chapters, but because a characteristically contemporary consideration of their meaning comes at the point where Christian identity is viewed as witness and service in the changing, buzzing, pluralistic world of the twentieth century. Faith, love and hope are individually and ecclesially Christian patterns of attitude and action, but they also bear profoundly on the Christian's and the Church's role in the world. Vatican II, which did not offer a revised or updated treatise on justification in continuity with the Council of Trent, certainly provided a powerful understanding of Christian identity and the supernatural virtues in its *Pastoral Constitution on the Church in the Modern World (Gaudium et Spes).* Here the issue is not the relation of the individual to the God who saves, but the relation of the Christian community and individual to the world of the twentieth century, a world of atheism, non-Christian religions, technology, and competing ideologies, a world which hungers for emancipation. Faith, love and hope are conceived in this document as profoundly social and liberating in their nature and scope.

In a social and emancipatory perspective, faith is not primarily intellectual or fiducial, but performative, and thus is inseparable from love.[28] Participation in God's truth or trust in the mercy of God yields pride of place to an understanding of faith which is informed by a knowledge of God's liberating deeds. This faith remembers that God created, ransomed, and blessed his people as *a people*. This faith gives special attention to the prophetic and apocalyptic traditions of Israel, which deeply criticize the evil status quo of king, priest, wealthy ruling class or idolatrous enemies in the name of the God who is totally committed to forming and preserving a covenantal people. A social and emancipatory love is rooted in this sense of God's commitment to a people of justice and peace. It is capable of acting and suffering in the present in identification with the marginal and the oppressed (the "widows, orphans and strangers in the land"), working for their benefit on the level of personal support and assistance, as well as creating new institutional structures of a political and economic kind so that justice does not depend on personal whim.

The primary thrust of performative faith and love and their dynamic orientation comes from hope, which in the First Letter to the Thessalonians is placed last in the series for several reasons. First, hope bears on the future dimension of faith and love. The experience of the liberating God in the lives of people in the past supports love's commitment to the present needs of people. Hope keeps open a future for both past fidelity and present love by allowing God to be the power of the future drawing the present and its past into God's future for us: a new heaven and a new earth. Hope is the God-given stance which is created by and open to the central mystery which prompts faith and love as well: Jesus Christ as the resurrection and life of the world. The recent "rediscovery" of hope by theologians such as Moltmann, Metz and Pannenberg[29] has allowed the resurrection of Jesus to come into its own as God's full-bodied promise to the world and human history: the future is the gift par excellence—the future, not as open possibility "up above" but the advent (in German, *Zukunft,* "coming toward") of God to our history which draws history toward its consummation as a Kingdom of justice and peace. The hope which bears performative faith and love into the future that depends on God's advent and graced human cooperation shows itself as hope in God for the world. And Christians evidence that hope in their witness and their service.

As authentic witnesses, Christians avoid any effort to force the issue, that is, to compel openness to that advent among other people. A contradictory notion if there ever was one: forced openness! Rather, Christians witness to the thoroughly human process of salvation and to the source of that process who is Christ in the power of the Spirit. The process of acceptance, conversion, community and serving love is the very unfolding of true human identity, always including graciousness as well as human involvement. Every person and every community is authentically human to the degree that they develop in response to "grace" or "gift" *in some form* in their lives. Even an atheistic Camus keeps far from idols and knows how to be grateful for the mystery of being human. A Buddhist, thinking in very different terms from a Christian, understands that wholeness comes not from self-assertion of the ego, but as uncanny gift of illumination which cannot be forced. Even on the psychiatrist's couch, the patient (who is paying handsomely) is experiencing healing partly because of the ambiance of acceptance and compassionate fidelity offered by the doctor which is not simply measurable by dollar signs! Grace in the sense of giftedness, however interpreted, is the horizon of true human development. Giftedness is the horizon of human life when well lived, even if the gift seems to come from the Silence or the Void. Within that horizon human life can blossom; the pattern is always similar in outline: interior acceptance coming from the other, empowering persons or communities to love and to give themselves to others. Thus Christian witness as witness to grace touches something basic to all human beings.

What makes the witness Christian, of course, is the proclamation of the source and goal and full dimension of the gift and the process as Christians experience it: God sharing the divine life through Christ in the Spirit. The life Christians live is not simply theirs but Christ's, or God's in Christ. The gift has a name and the process has a future which has revealed its countenance and anchored their hopes. Christians rejoice in the revelation of the ultimate source of the gift (God as "Abba," as absolutely near) and rejoice as well in the revelation of authentic humanity as rooted in the

Gift (Jesus Christ as the New Creation). Christians hope that all others may come to share that good news, but often hope more realistically that their witness may help others deepen in their own sense of gift, however they may name that gift or even refuse to give that dimension of their lives a name.

Service is the second way that Christian identity expresses itself in the world. Grace frees people more and more from crippling forms of self-concern, from sin, legalism and death in its various forms of willful isolation. To the extent that self-justification and self-maintenance cease to be vital needs of the self, the Christian individual or community can be touched by the needs of others, suffer their sufferings in patient love, and respond out of their resources and out of the abundance of the resource that is Christ's presence effective through them. This service takes not only the form of good deeds done for individuals but service to institutions as well, which leads us to the concept of social grace.

Social Grace

The individual human person will always have a privileged role in any Christian theology of grace. The person is the place where justification and sanctification, virtue and sin exist in the full sense, that is, exist as freely accepted realities. Ultimately, each person is responsible to God for his or her own life, including, of course, the relationships which make up so much of a person's life. Again, each person is an absolute value and cannot be simply fit into a system or organization of which he or she would be only a part, element or function. The individual is irreducible to any system.

On the other hand, the individual human person is nourished or hindered by the web of relationships which make up the social dimension of life. The family is the primary instance of a web of relationships which helps to fashion who a person will become. The particular family we were born into was the fruit of the decision of our father and mother to marry and have children. To a certain extent—but one not easily determinable—our families were the kind they were because of people's choices. But in other equally important ways, they were fashioned by the culture's view of what a family should be like, as well as the view of marriage and family offered by the Catholic Church.

There were aspects of our family life which expressed the love and generosity of our parents for us. These aspects were both unpredictable actions on the part of our parents and habitual ways of acting which made up the normal, regular course of our living together as family. Much of the care shown us during our early years was of this consistent, regular kind: basic things like regular, nourishing meals offered at predictable times, perhaps the pattern of spending time together after dinner, a well-kept apartment or house which nourished a sense of security and well-being. These routinized forms of relationship, insofar as they were expressions of real care and love, would be called, in contemporary language, social grace.

But there is another side to social grace as well. These routines tended to form us and incline us to good habits; for example, we learned to treat ourselves and the other members of our families with respect and caring love. As a social support of our personal love and care and concern for others our families functioned as social grace.

This simple example suggests that social grace is not some "thing" existing all by itself "out there." Like all grace, it is related to human freedom primarily, either as an effect of graced freedom or supporting and aiding graced freedom, which is always essentially personal freedom.

Social grace is a new concept in the sense that in the twentieth century our explicit consciousness of society and social organizations is more nuanced and complex than that of previous centuries, and so the Christian understanding of grace is now able to receive more attention precisely as a social reality. But it would be wrong to see the development of the notion of social grace as deriving simply from the emergence of sociology and historical consciousness. Christians have returned to the record of salvation history in both the Old and New Testament and have come to a renewed appreciation of the social forms of grace in both Testaments. Israel and the Church are the primary instances of social grace for any theology of grace. In the history of theology, moreover, the notion of sacramental grace as well as of habitual grace foreshadowed the contemporary notion. Sacramental grace is ecclesial grace—grace which is caused symbolically by the Church expressing its responsive identity in relation to the presence of Christ. While its formal effect is the sanctification of those who are receiving the sacrament, the institutional aspects of the sacrament in its social setting lend support to the grace being offered and give expression to that grace. It is not always easy to perceive the sacrament of anointing of the sick as a social grace when the priest and the patient are the only ones involved in a public way. But when a small gathering of believers participates in the celebration, then it becomes apparent that this sacrament is indeed social, as well as personal grace.

In the classical theology of grace, a distinction—still valid— was made between a habit and an act. A habit is a permanent disposition residing in a person which facilitates certain kinds of actions. Grace is habitual when it elevates human nature, giving it the ability to perform activities proportionate to its supernatural goal. In modern terms, habitual grace is a personal, supernatural structure which makes possible and indeed facilitates gracious choices and actions. This distinction between habit and acts in the personal realm can be transposed to the social realm, where institutional routines can serve gracious living as expressed in acts of love of God and neighbor. As Roger Haight puts it: "May we not say that the goal or purpose of grace in this world is to build more and more institutions that incarnate, mediate and foster in the world the effects of grace, namely, forgiveness, self-transcending love, communities of reconciliation and concern? And if this is the case, is not this an expression of the goal of history under the influence of grace?"[30]

6 Prospects for the Theology of Grace

In the preceding chapters we have seen a pattern of grace at work in the lives of Christians. Spreading the pattern out under the names employed in this book was a way of presenting some of the elements of a contemporary theology of grace. The exposition has tried to be introductory in nature while at the same time taking into account basic themes of recent theologians who have written on this topic.

The theology of grace is of interest to theologians of the present day as much as it has ever been, but the form of the interest has changed. A course in the theology of grace now could very likely bear the title "Theological Anthropology" to express the fact that a theological approach to grace is really an approach to the religious meaning of the human person and human society. Moreover, as I hope has been made clear in the course of the previous chapters, much of today's theologizing about grace is found in Christology and ecclesiology. Theologians appreciate the fact that grace is concrete, not an abstraction. We come to know grace through its expressions, its signs and symbols. Because grace is embodied, theologians prefer to reflect on its nature and meaning in connection with the bodily realities which render grace present and effective in the world: Jesus and the Church.[31] What are some areas in the theology of grace where we can expect further development in the coming years? That is the question which this chapter will treat: some prospects for the theology of grace.

Religious Experience

If grace is not a separate item within our field of experience, as authors such as Rahner maintain, then grace is present as part and parcel of all turning points, exchanges of life between people and groups and people and nature, in all times of painful change and quiet fidelity. The offer of grace is a constant but its recognition can be sporadic, and as people become more alert to its presence the Christian community will develop a greater sensitivity to the endless concrete shapes grace can adopt. For this reason theologians will turn to people's religious experience more often in order to learn about how God's grace works in human lives.

Recently we have seen much attention given to narrative theology, a form of theology which takes story as a fundamental way of expressing God's love and its effects in human lives. In the past, the lives of the saints played a very important role in the spiritual lives of Christians, and the Gospel narratives of Jesus have always been at the center of both public worship and many people's spiritual lives. But we are going to see, I think, more and more stories of ordinary people's experiences of God made available to the community, as they come to recognize God's communication with them through the web of their family, work, recreation and politics. To the extent that they do experience God as part of their "ordinary" lives and come to deepen that experience and learn how to tell the story of that experience, the whole Church will be enriched by the telling.[32]

The context which helps people learn and tell the story of their relationship with God can be the parish, or a voluntary association of Christians meeting for worship, prayer or collective social action. In Latin America the *communidades de base* have provided this kind of nurturing atmosphere in recent years. By providing a context in which the Word of God could be heard as a Word addressed to the members' daily lives, these communities help people experience their painful and hopeful assumption of political responsibility for themselves and others as an experience of grace.[33]

A particularly helpful aid for the nurturing of this alertness is the practice of spiritual direction, whether one-to-one or in groups. The phrase "spiritual direction" means different things to different people, but I use the term to refer to a relationship in which an individual or group helps another or others to develop the ability to hear God's Word through the concrete stuff of their lives, to be aware of their spontaneous reactions to that Word, and to learn to respond freely to it. The emphasis falls on the relation between God and the person, God and the group, and not, as in counseling, between or among the human beings. God is the real director, and the "spiritual director" is the companion or peer who helps the praying people to be real before God and to let God be real for them. The stories of grace which emerge from this kind of growth in real prayer will increasingly become part of the theology of the grace of Christ.[34]

The theology of grace, as classically developed, was long on argument and short on narrative. In the future, one can hope, narrative and critical reflection will each find guidance and nourishment in the other.

Grace and Liberation

Prayer is not a half-hour a day enterprise but the developing alertness and responsiveness to God's presence in and through the rhythms, the pressures, the joys, the grind and the breakthroughs of ordinary living. Nor is prayer simply the activity of an individual with his or her God. Prayer—alertness and responsiveness to God's presence in human life—is a *social* and *political* reality as well. When people experience themselves as companions and members of each other, and come to know God and the divine call to them more sharply in that experience, then they are experiencing grace as a power which incorporates, which makes a body of unity where before there was fragmentation and isolation. And when people experience their participation in the *polis* as a vital dimension of their relationship to God—again, not as a matter of theory but of actual experience—they are offering material for a public theology or a liberation theology, or a theology of first-world Christianity. The experience of social grace and political grace is rooted in both individuals and in groups, but it remains implicit and thus not instructive until it becomes the stuff of story-telling and critical reflection. When they do come to the surface, these experiences can encourage and nurture people as they assume political responsibility —which is always costly—and struggle for more just social structures and more equitable political processes.

As women grow in the sense of their changing roles in society and Church, their experience of God is changing as well, and it will be important to both them and the larger community of believers that they tell the story of their struggle for freedom and new relationships as a story of the experienced presence and absence of God. There is already a growing body of literature about women's stories as journeys with God and their sisters which needs to be welcomed into a renewed theology of grace for the good of women and men.

As we move into a new age, beyond patriarchy, how will grace be experienced and named by both men and women?[35] What happens to their experience of grace when men, in middle life, become more sensitive to the feminine side of their psyche, and when women become more attuned to their need to assert themselves and to learn a healthy autonomy and responsibility for their lives? The learning which results from the changes in people's lives such as middle life does not simply provide documentation for an already developed theory of grace, but can help shape the very understanding of grace in the Christian community. The more we learn about the psychological "laws" of personal maturation and community development, and the better we understand how beneficial social change occurs, the more theologians can test out their basic theorem that God's grace is both a humanizing and divinizing influence in people's lives.

On the other hand, psychological and social dynamics are not identical with grace as such. The conscious and unconscious aspects of human personality contain of themselves enormous resources for healing, change and maturation. These resources are part of human nature and are not grace in the sense of God's self-communication or the formal effects of that self-communication. Roger Haight recently criticized Juan Luis Segundo for inaccurately attributing a certain psychological phenomenon to grace.[36] In his *Grace and the Human Condition,*[37] Juan Luis Segundo maintained that grace is needed for the personalization of our lives, for this is a process contrary to the law of least resistance which otherwise rules our nature. In other words, he contends that without grace, human freedom would not be able to develop and people would slip back more and more into a "thing-like" existence. Haight points out that with deliberation and by developing a sense of responsibility, a person or a group *can* put a personal stamp on what before was something simply happening to them. All forms of psychotherapy and social reform are predicated on this assumption of human capability. Saving grace is not strictly necessary in this sphere. Grace is indeed everywhere, but not every aspect of human maturation requires grace for its occurrence.

But having said this, the point is not to separate the psychological and the "gracious" but to realize that there is need for much more effort in relating psychology and the theology of grace. A beginning has been made. Some years ago a Catholic psychiatrist, William Meissner, published an anthology and commentary on the foundations for a psychology of grace.[38] More recently, Professor Tom Driver of Union Theological Seminary wrote a charming series of reflections on the "patterns of grace" using some ideas from Gestalt therapy and his own experience and theological wisdom.[39] And a wise psychiatrist, Gerald May, who is also an able spiritual director, published an excellent introduction to contemplative psychology, which is very sensitive to the relation between grace and psyche.[40]

In and through psychological suffering, conflict, breakthroughs and growth, God's grace makes itself known. For grace is God's gifting us with forgiveness and divine life—the two fundamental blessings of the Kingdom—and both gifts are for the restoration and consummation of human beings and the material world through humans. The "Godwardness" of human experience and the "Christwardness" of all human community are the stuff of grace, and all psychological development and retardation affect the quality of relationship to God and the quality of membership in the living body of Christ. So we can expect more interaction between psychology and theology precisely in these areas of healing and development where the creaturely resources of human beings are experienced as intertwined with God's gift.

Grace and Material Creation

A decade ago, Professor Joseph Sittler of the Divinity School of the University of Chicago wrote a book which called for a whole new approach to the theology of grace which, while drawing on the riches of the tradition, would take seriously the new relationships of human beings to nature and to material creation. For too long, grace in many Christian traditions had been considered only as an element in the couple "grace-sin" and as a reality impinging upon human beings as an almost self-contained sphere of being. Sittler wonders how the material universe, which helps constitute human beings in their living identity, can be left out of the consummation of humanity which God is bringing about in Christ. Referring to Paul's famous passage in Romans 8:19-25, he asks how some theologians can restrict the application of this text about creation's groaning to human history, and not appreciate its reference to material creation as well.[41]

Nature, or the material creation as such, does not cause grace, Sittler reminds us, any more than transactions among people cause grace. The cause, source of origin of grace is God alone, through Christ and in the Spirit. But *all* relationships between humanity and nature can be occasions of grace, in Sittler's terms, or symbolic causes (expressions) of grace, in Catholic terms.

The image of the closed universe, which excludes involvement by a "higher power," is the image of classical physics, whose domain is that of sensory experience and whose model is that of the machine. The microcosmic and the macrocosmic worlds of quantum mechanics and relativity theory are not closed in that sense, but more than tinged with mystery. Moreover, the differences and affinity between conciousness and nature suggest to thinkers like Teilhard de Chardin that self-transcendence is not foreign to the universe but its energizing key; in humans that self-transcendence has become conscious of itself. Grace is not a foreign element thrown into a self-contained, consistent universe, an unnecessary or arbitrary superstructure, but the dynamism for the sake of which the kind of universe disclosed by contemporary science is at work. As science learns to treat consciousness on its own terms instead of reducing it to nerve endings and brain cells, it becomes clearer even for scientists that in and through the "miracle" of human awareness, matter acquires purpose, goals and definition. God's grace receives cooperation or frustration from the universe to the extent that human beings interact with material creation as stewards and participants in God's loving creation of nature, or fail to do so, treating matter and nature simply as the enemy to be strangled, degraded, used up.[42]

What *is* the relationship between grace and science, grace and technology? More pointedly, what is the connection between God's grace and the nuclear arms race or nuclear disarmament? These questions are ethical in nature, to be sure, but they, at root, have everything to do with people's experience or lack of experience of grace. Whence comes people's basic sense of security, which would allow them to take risks for peace? Is that source reliable, more powerful than the threatening forces in their lives? What kinds of "membering" experiences have people known? Are foreigners sensed as the enemy, the outsiders who have no claim on "us"? The images we nourish about "us" and "them" are images of grace or images of sin. Images such as these help shape people's decisions regarding how they will employ technology, either as an instrument of fear or as a prolongation of God's good creation.

The theology of grace, like the very experience of grace, is in its early stages. So much more remains to be learned. For

> "from his fullness have we all received,
> grace upon grace" (Jn 1:16).

Notes

1. Erik Erickson, *Childhood and Society,* 2nd ed. (New York: Norton, 1963); *Identity, Youth and Crisis* (New York: Norton, 1968); *Insight and Responsibility* (London: Faber, 1964); Lawrence Kohlberg, *The Philosophy of Moral Development* (San Francisco: Harper and Row, 1981); Daniel J. Levinson, *The Seasons of a Man's Life* (New York: Ballantine, 1978); Donald Evans, *Struggle and Fulfillment: The Inner Dynamics of Religion and Morality* (New York: Collins, 1979); James Fowler, *Stages of Faith: The Psychology of Human Development and the Quest for Meaning* (San Francisco: Harper and Row, 1981); Carol Gilligan, *In a Different Voice: Psychological Theory and Women's Development* (Cambridge: Harvard University Press, 1982); Robert Kegan, *The Evolving Self: Problem and Process in Human Development* (Cambridge: Harvard University Press, 1982).

2. *The Search for God in Time and Memory* (Notre Dame: University of Notre Dame, 1977), Ch. 1.

3. *The Denial of Death* (New York: The Free Press, 1973).

4. *Method in Theology* (New York: Herder and Herder, 1972), p. xi.

5. "Basic Theological Interpretation of the Second Vatican Council," in *Concern for the Church,* trans. by Edward Quinn (New York: Crossroad, 1981), pp. 77-89.

6. *Foundations of Christian Faith: An Introduction to the Idea of Christianity,* trans. by William V. Dych (New York: Seabury, 1978), pp. 116-137.

7. "Reflections on the Experience of Grace," *Theological Investigations,* Vol. 3, trans. by Karl-H. and Boniface Kruger (New York: Seabury, 1974), pp. 86-90.

8. *Hearers of the Word,* trans. by Michael Richards (New York: Herder and Herder, 1969), p. 106.

9. *The Crucified Jesus Is No Stranger* (New York: Seabury, 1977).

10. New York: Nelson, 1964.

11. Frans Jozef van Beeck treats both Jesus' and Christians' identity as a rhetoric of inclusion in his *Christ Proclaimed: Christology as Rhetoric* (New York: Paulist, 1979).

12. *The Crucified Jesus Is No Stranger,* pp. 100f.

13. Sebastian Moore and Edward Schillebeeckx both stress the conversion aspect of the Easter experience. See Moore, *The Fire and the Rose Are One* (New York: Seabury, 1980), and Schillebeeckx, *Jesus: An Experiment in Christology,* trans by Hubert Hoskins (New York: Seabury, 1979).

14. Trans. by E. Buchanan (Boston: Beacon Press, 1969), pp. 3-24.

15. *Vorfragen zu einem okumenischen Amtsverstandnis* (Freiburg: Herder, 1974).

16. *Christ: The Experience of Jesus as Lord,* trans. by John Bowden (New York: Crossroad, 1980).

17. *Interim Report on the Books Jesus and Christ,* trans. by John Bowden (New York: Crossroad, 1981), pp. 126ff.

18. *Ibid.,* p. 95.

19. *The Charismatic Leader and His Followers,* trans. by James Greig (New York: Crossroad, 1981).

20. Raymond Brown, *Jesus, God and Man: Modern Biblical Reflections* (New York: Macmillan, 1967), pp. 23-38.

21. *Christ Proclaimed, passim.*

22. *Christian at the Crossroad,* trans. by V. Green (New York: Crossroad, 1975), pp. 62-69.

23. "The Logic of Concrete Individual Knowledge in Ignatius Loyola," in *The Dynamic Element in the Church,* trans. by W.J. O'Hara (New York: Herder and Herder, 1964), pp. 84-170.

24. "Institution and Charisma in the Church" in *A Church To Believe In* (New York: Crossroad, 1982), pp. 19-40.

25. *Christ Proclaimed,* pp. 137-141.

26. See Karl Rahner, "The One Christ and the Universality of Salvation," in *Theological Investigations,* Vol. 16, trans. by David Morland (New York: Crossroad, 1979), pp. 207-216.

27. *Christ Proclaimed,* Ch. 11.

28. Avery Dulles, "The Meaning of Faith Considered in Relationship to Justice," in J. C. Haughey, ed., *The Faith That Does Justice* (New York: Paulist, 1977), pp. 10-46.

29. Jurgen Moltmann, *The Theology of Hope,* trans. by J. Leitch (New York: Harper and Row, 1967); Wolfhart Pannenberg, *Jesus: God and Man,* trans. by D. Priebe (Philadelphia: Westminster, 1968).

30. *The Experience and Language of Grace* (New York: Paulist, 1979), p. 181.

31. Gisbert Greshake, in his scholarly volume *Gnade als konkrete Freiheit: eine Untersuchung zur Gnadelehre des Pelagius* (Mainz: Matthias-Grunewald Verlag, 1972), shows how St. Augustine's victory over Pelagius led the Church to stress the invisible dimensions of grace over the public and social aspects.

32. Two fine examples of such narration are Frederick Buechner's *Sacred Journey* (San Francisco: Harper, 1982) and the sequel, *Now and Then* (San Francisco: Harper, 1983).

33. Ernesto Cardenal, *The Gospel in Solentiname,* trans. by Donald D. Walsh (Maryknoll, N.Y.: Orbis, 1976).

34. William A. Barry and William J. Connolly, *The Practice of Spiritual Direction* (New York: Seabury, 1982).

35. See Beatrice Bruteau, "Neo-Feminism and the Next Evolution in Consciousness," *Cross Currents* 27 (1977), 170-182; also Judith Plaskow, *Sex, Sin and Grace: Women's Experience in the Theologies of Reinhold Niebuhr and Paul Tillich* (Washington, D.C.: University Press of America, 1980).

36. *The Experience and Language of Grace,* pp. 52f., nn. 20 and 23.

37. *Grace and the Human Condition* (Maryknoll, N.Y.: Orbis, 1973), Ch. 1.

38. *Foundations for a Psychology of Grace* (Glen Rock, N.J.: Paulist, 1966).

39. *Patterns of Grace: Human Experience as Word of God* (San Francisco: Harper, 1977).

40. *Will and Spirit: A Contemplative Psychology* (San Francisco: Harper and Row, 1982).

41. *Essays on Nature and Grace* (Philadelphia: Fortress, 1972), pp. 108f.

42. See Zachary Hayes, O.F.M., *What Are They Saying About Creation?* (New York: Paulist, 1980).

Selected Bibliography

1. Ernest Becker, *The Denial of Death* (New York: The Free Press, 1973).
2. Frederick Buechner, *Sacred Journey* (San Francisco: Harper, 1982) and the sequel, *Now and Then* (San Francisco: Harper, 1983).
3. Tom F. Driver, *Patterns of Grace: Human Experience as Word of God* (San Francisco: Harper, 1977).
4. Roger Haight, *The Experience and Language of Grace* (New York: Paulist, 1979).
5. Hans Kung, *Justification* (New York: Nelson, 1964).
6. Gerald May, *Will and Spirit: A Contemplative Psychology* (San Francisco: Harper and Row, 1982).
7. William Meissner, *Foundations for a Psychology of Grace* (Glen Rock, N.J.: Paulist, 1966).
8. Sebastian Moore, *The Crucified Jesus Is No Stranger* (New York: Seabury, 1977).
9. Sebastian Moore, *The Fire and the Rose Are One* (New York: Seabury, 1980).
10. Leo J. O'Donovan, *A World of Grace: An Introduction to the Themes and Foundations of Karl Rahner's Theology* (New York: Crossroad, 1980).
11. Judith Plaskow, *Sex, Sin and Grace: Women's Experience in the Theologies of Reinhold Niebuhr and Paul Tillich* (Washington, D.C.: University Press of America, 1980).
12. Karl Rahner, *Foundations of Christian Faith: An Introduction to the Idea of Christianity,* trans. by William V. Dych (New York: Seabury, 1974).
13. Karl Rahner, *Christian at the Crossroad,* trans. by V. Green (New York: Crossroad, 1975).
14. Edward Schillebeeckx, *Christ: The Experience of Jesus as Lord,* trans, by John Bowden (New York: Crossroad, 1980).
15. Juan Luis Segundo, *Grace and the Human Condition* (Maryknoll, N.Y.: Orbis, 1973).
16. Joseph Sittler, *Essays on Nature and Grace* (Philadelphia: Fortress, 1972).

Other Books in this Series

What are they saying about Mysticism? *by Harvey D. Egan, S.J.*

What are they saying about Christ and World Religions?
by Lucien Richard, O.M.I.

What are they saying about the Trinity? *by Joseph A. Bracken, S.J.*

What are they saying about non-Christian Faith?
by Denise Lardner Carmody

What are they saying about Christian-Jewish Relations?
by John T. Pawlikowski

What are they saying about the Resurrection? *by Gerald O'Collins*

What are they saying about Creation? *by Zachary Hayes, O.F.M.*

What are they saying about the Prophets? *by David P. Reid, SS.CC.*

What are they saying about Moral Norms? *by Richard M. Gula, S.S.*

What are they saying about Death and Christian Hope?
by Monika Hellwig

What are they saying about Sexual Morality? *by James P. Hanigan*

What are they saying about Jesus? *by Gerald O'Collins*

What are they saying about Dogma? *by William E. Reiser, S.J.*

What are they saying about Luke and Acts?
by Robert J. Karris, O.F.M.

What are they saying about Peace and War? *by Thomas A. Shannon*

What are they saying about Papal Primacy?
by J. Michael Miller, C.S.B.

What are they saying about Matthew? *by Donald Senior, C.P.*

What are they saying about the End of the World?
by Zachary Hayes, O.F.M.

What are they saying about Wisdom Literature?
by Dianne Bergant, C.S.A.